The Mortified Christian

Showing the Nature, Signs, Necessity, and Difficulty of True Mortification

with

The Right Hearing of Sermons

by

Christopher Love
Minister of St. Lawrence Jewry, London

Edited by Rev. Don Kistler

Soli Deo Gloria Publications
. . . for instruction in righteousness . . .

Soli Deo Gloria Publications
P.O. Box 451, Morgan, PA 15064
(412) 221-1901/FAX 221-1902

*

*

ISBN 1-57358-078-3

EDITOR'S NOTE: These sermons were originally delivered verbally and transcribed in shorthand before being published. The author of them tended to reinforce his points by review and repetition. It will help the reader to think of himself as a parishioner hearing these sermons.

Contents

The Mortified Christian

The Right Hearing of Sermons

To the Reader

The author of these treatises is sufficiently known and approved; his works praise him in the gates. He was indeed a workman who needed not to be ashamed. He was not a blazing comet to show his own parts, but a genuine star to lead men to Christ.

It is the unhappiness of our age that men desire rather to have their ears tickled than their hearts affected. It is the sin of many jingling preachers that they mind rather the humoring of their hearers' fancies than the saving of their souls, little considering that saying of Seneca: "Sick men are not bettered by physicians' sugared words, but by their skillful hands." Such a one was not the reverend author of these sermons. We who had the happiness to be better acquainted with him can truly say that he did not preach himself, but Jesus Christ his Lord, and himself the church's servant for Jesus' sake.

Here are presented to you old doctrines which will not gratify that itch of novelty which has now become epidemic. Here are common doctrines which will not humor that affected singularity of which most men are sick. Here are plain doctrines that will not comply with the curious palates of this wanton age. However, remember that counsel of the prophet: inquire for the good old paths so you shall find rest for your soul. It may be that you have wandered through all the points of the compass, and have perceived in yourself nothing but disquiet and unsettledness. It will, therefore, be your wisdom to return to the right point, to come to your first husband, for then it was better with you than now. Here you will find if not pleasure, yet nourishment. If your palate is not pleased, your heart may be bettered if you do not willfully hinder it.

These sermons concern mortification, in which the author's judgment is more to be valued because his heart was a commentary upon his text, and his own experience was a seal to his doctrine.

We have only this to add: these sermons are not irregular births, but have been either collected out of or compared with his own notes, and taken from his own mouth by the pen of a ready writer. Our desire is that you would candidly accept them, diligently read them, and conscientiously practice those great duties that are here pressed. As this will tend to the comfort of your own soul at that great day of account; so it will exceedingly refresh and encourage your servants in the work of the gospel:

Edmund Calamy
Jeremiah Whitaker
Matthew Poole
Simeon Ashe
William Taylor

Sermon 1

"For if ye live after the flesh, ye shall die, but if ye through the Spirit do mortify the deeds of the body, ye shall live." Romans 8:13

The Text Opened

Moses said to Israel in Deuteronomy 30:19, "I have set before you life and death, blessing and cursing; therefore choose life, that both thou and thy seed may live." This is the sum and scope of the subject I am now to treat, a treatise that may not only invite, but crave your serious attention and consideration, for they are matters of great concern of life and death. If you live after the flesh you shall die, but if you, through the Spirit, mortify the deeds of the body, you shall live.

The chapter out of which my text is taken contains in it the great charter of a Christian, wherein are enrolled the many privileges of believers. And yet among them, here and there, are mingled and interspersed many fearful threatenings and denunciations. Among these, one is in my text: "If you live after the flesh, you shall die." I shall not stand long upon the explication of the words, as they are very plain and obvious to the weakest capacity.

"If you live after the flesh." All men who are alive live *in* the flesh, but no man should live *after* the flesh. To live after the flesh, that is, after the sinful motions and corrupt dictates of nature, implies these three things:

1. Continuance and constancy in a way of sin. It is not said "if you *do* after the flesh you shall die," for the best of God's children do. Yet they do not *live* after the flesh; they do not make a trade of sin. To live after the flesh signifies a continued act of sin.

2. It notes not only constancy and continuance, but also complacence and delight in sin. Men are wont to rejoice in life; and so to live after the flesh implies a delight and complacency in sin.

3. It implies a great deal of industry and labor in the ways of sin. It is one thing for sin to follow after you, and another thing for you to follow after sin. The Apostle says in Galatians 6:1: "Brethren, if any man be overtaken in a fault, ye which are spiritual, restore such a one with the spirit of meekness." Sin runs after a godly man and overtakes him, but a wicked man runs after sin and overtakes sin. It is one thing for corruption to dog you, and another thing for you to run after sin and satisfy the desires of the flesh and of the mind. To live after the flesh denotes constancy, complacency, and industry in the ways of sin.

The corrupt dictates and motions of the body are called "flesh" for these reasons:

First, because sin is in the flesh as well as in the spirit; the members of the body are corrupt as well as the soul (James 4:1).

Second, because sin is naturally as dear to a man as his own flesh, and hence it is compared to the right eye and the right hand.

Third, because sin is acted out by the flesh, and

that being the instrument of acting out sin it is called by its name. Sin was in us as soon as we put on flesh, and will be in us as long as we live in the flesh. As David says in Psalm 51:5, "I was shaped in iniquity, and in sin did my mother conceive me." Sin will remain in us as long as we live in this world.

If you live after the flesh, you shall die. Die! That is good news. It would be well for a man who takes his swing in sinful delights and pleasures that he might die like a beast, that there might be an end of him. But this must not be understood as if the soul should die eternally, but you shall die, that is, you shall incur damnation if you live after the flesh.

OBJECTION. But some may ask how the Apostle could say that those who live after the flesh shall die, whereas the damned in hellfire shall live in those torments perpetually (Mark 9:44).

ANSWER. Though the wicked shall live in hell, their damnation is called a "death" for two reasons. In Scripture phrase, that does not deserve the name of "life" that does not bring comfort with it; and the Scripture expresses a doleful and dismal estate by the name of death. Also, it is called death because these persons are estranged and separated from God who is life.

"If you live after the flesh you shall die, but if ye through the Spirit do mortify the deeds of the body, you shall live." You may sin by your own strength; but you cannot mortify sin but by the strength of the Spirit.

"Mortify the deeds of the body," means to keep under and subdue the power and predominance of sin. If you mortify the deeds of the body, that is, those sins that are acted in the body, then you shall live—not everlastingly here, but you shall live forever in heaven, and you shall be saved. This is that indispensable condition upon which God has entailed salvation: If you, through the Spirit mortify the deeds of the body you shall live.

Now, having thus opened the words, I once more say to you as did Moses to Israel: "Behold, I have set before you this day blessing and cursing, life and death; therefore choose which you will have." I have set before you life: if you through the Spirit mortify the deeds of the body, you shall live. And I have set before you death: if you live after the flesh you shall die. Therefore, choose whether you will be saved or damned, whether you will live or die.

The great scope of the Apostle in this chapter is to stir up and press believers to walk as ones worthy of their justification. Though Christ does all for us in point of justification, we must do something, too. Though Christ justifies us from the *guilt* of sin, we must labor to be freed from the *filth* of sin. This exhortation the Apostle presses upon them by three arguments:

1. Romans 8:12: "Brethren, we are debtors, not to the flesh, to live after the flesh"; no, we are debtors to the Spirit, to live after the Spirit. We are indebted to God to mortify our sins and corruptions; and it's a part of equity and common honesty to pay what we owe.

2. He presses it upon them by the sad consequence of their not walking as worthy of their justification: "if you live after the flesh you shall die."

3. He presses them to it by the great benefit and

advantage that will redound to them upon the performance of this duty: "if you through the Spirit mortify the deeds of the body, you shall live."

Before I come to the distinct handling of the words and insist upon those points I intend principally to speak of, I shall, from the general view and aspect of the text, draw out eight doctrinal considerations, so that you may see the strength of the text and how many observations this short text will afford. I will only name them.

CONSIDERATION 1. This is drawn from the consideration of the persons to whom Paul wrote: they were not wicked men only, such as were in a state of paganism, unbelievers, but those also who were in a converted state, true believers. To these Paul uses this denunciation. From whence I note:

DOCTRINE 1. Denunciations and threatenings are to be pressed upon converted as well as unconverted men.

It is observable that the Word of God is not only compared in 1 Peter 2:2 to milk, which is of a pleasant taste, but it is likewise compared to salt in Colossians 4:6. For the godly have a great deal of rottenness and corruption in them which must be eaten out by the salt of the Word; and they thereby are kept pure and spotless.

CONSIDERATION 2. The Apostle not only preaches comfort to believers, justification to them, that there is "no condemnation to those who are in Christ Jesus" (Romans 8:1), but he likewise preaches threatenings to them. From whence observe:

DOCTRINE 2. Doctrines of terror ought to be pressed upon believers as well as doctrines of com-

fort and consolation.

Therefore, they only preach half the will of God who only handle doctrines of comfort, and never press men to duty and encourage men to the practice of godliness.

CONSIDERATION 3. The Apostle not only preaches terror and denunciations, but he also joins these threatening doctrines of comfort. From whence observe further:

DOCTRINE 3. When ministers preach doctrines of terror and condemnation, they ought to mingle with them doctrines of comfort and consolation.

Therefore, as they are to blame who always preach doctrines of comfort, so likewise they are blameworthy who *never* preach comfort. A variety of doctrine sets off a man's ministry with a greater luster, beauty, and efficacy upon the hearts of the hearers.

CONSIDERATION 4. Note the method the Apostle uses here: he first preaches terror before he preaches doctrines of comfort. "If you live after the flesh you shall die, but if you through the Spirit do mortify the deeds of the body, you shall live." From whence we may observe this doctrine:

DOCTRINE 4. When Christians grow sensual, wanton, careless, and remiss in duties, laying aside that holy watchfulness and care they were wont to have, at such times as these doctrines of terror are more needful and necessary than doctrines of comfort.

CONSIDERATION 5. This is drawn from the addition of the phrase in the text, "through the Spirit." The former part of the verse does not say, "If ye through the power of the devil do live after the flesh, ye shall die"; but here these words are added, "If you through the Spirit." From whence observe:

DOCTRINE 5. A man may commit sin by his own strength, but he cannot mortify sin but by the help of the Spirit.

A single man can as soon destroy a whole army of men with his own hand as subdue one sin by his own power. Any man may wound himself, but every man cannot heal himself. You may commit sin, but you cannot purge out sin. A man may easily run down a hill, but it is very difficult getting up a hill. A man may easily commit sin, but he cannot mortify sin except by the strength of the Spirit.

CONSIDERATION 6. "If you through the Spirit do mortify the deeds of the flesh." Observe that:

DOCTRINE 6. In every regenerate man there are some deeds and reminders and relics of sin and corruption still left.

CONSIDERATION 7. From the same phrase we may learn:

DOCTRINE 7. Christians stand in need of mortification as well as other men.

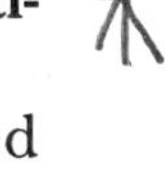

They have some unbridled passion or untamed affection or unruly lust that needs to be tamed as well as other men.

Godly men need sometimes to be tamed and hampered and mortified as well as the worst of men in the world.

CONSIDERATION 8. Last, we may observe from these words this doctrinal conclusion:

DOCTRINE 8. Men may expect their condition in another world to be answerable to what their carriage

and conversation is in this world.

Are you a man who gives way to the vain and sinful desires and corrupt motions of your own heart? Let me tell you that as surely as you are alive this day, if you continue and go on in this course you shall die, be damned, and be undone forever.

If you live after the flesh, you shall die, but if you are a man who labors to bridle and keep under your unruly lusts and untamed affections, so that grace may get the victory over your corruptions and so that sin may not rule and reign in your mortal bodies, you are on the ready way to obtaining life everlasting. Therefore I beseech you, my brethren, do not think or reason in this way with yourselves: "If I shall be saved, I shall be saved, though I live never so profanely; and if I shall be damned, I shall be damned, let me do what I will to the contrary." Do not argue this way, for here you see the Scripture tells you expressly that if you live after the flesh you shall die, but if you through the Spirit do mortify the deeds of the body, you shall live.

I have given you these eight doctrinal conclusions from the general scope and aspect of the words. I shall now draw out three more doctrines which I intend to insist upon.

"If you live after the flesh you shall die." From this phrase observe:

DOCTRINE 1. Living according to the world after the sinful motions and corrupt dictates of nature, without laboring to mortify and subdue them, is what will bring men to death and damnation.

I add this phrase in the doctrine: "without laboring to mortify and subdue them." Living after the flesh is put in opposition to mortifying the deeds of the flesh. If you live after the flesh without endeavoring to mortify and subdue the motions of it, this will bring you to death and damnation. Galatians 6:8: "He that soweth to the flesh shall of the flesh reap corruption; but he that soweth to the Spirit shall of the Spirit reap life everlasting." By "sowing to the flesh" is meant following after the desire of the flesh, and such as do this shall thereby reap damnation. You who have your seed time in sin shall have your harvest in hell. You shall inherit damnation and hellfire forever. If you sow to the flesh, you shall of the flesh reap corruption.

I shall speak to this doctrine only in this one sermon, because my intentions are principally to insist upon the other branch of the text: "if ye through the Spirit do mortify the deeds of the body, ye shall live." Therefore, I shall only answer one query, and then give you a practical use.

QUESTION. Some may say, "If it is so that those who live after the flesh must die, then how may I know and be assured and satisfied in my own conscience that I am a man who lives after the flesh, and that sin is not subdued and mortified in my soul?"

ANSWER. I shall give you six general means how you may know whether sin is unmortified in you or not, by your carriage both before and after the commission of any sin.

First, by your carriage before the commission of any sin. When there is a longing and hankering desire in your soul to commit sin, and a studying and contriving how to act, hereby the Scripture describes an unmortified man. Psalm 36:4: "He deviseth mischief upon his bed; he setteth himself in a way that is not good." When a man studies and contrives how to act out a sin and carry it out quietly and secretly, this is an argument (when upon such deliberate debates and rational consultations, a man sets himself in a way that is not good) that he has an unmortified heart. Therefore, if you plot, study, and contrive how to commit sin, it is a strong argument that the power of sin is not subdued and mortified in you.

Second, a corruption is unmortified in the soul when a man is more eager to commit the sin to which he is tempted than he is to resist it; when a man is all on fire, as it were, and so eager in the pursuit of a lust to the satisfaction of which he is tempted, that he casts away all thoughts of resistance. This argues such a man to have an unmortified heart. A godly man who has the power of mortifying grace upon his heart may fall into the same sins as you do, yet he encounters them, and takes more care how to resist sin than to act it out. Now, it may be, all your thoughts are taken up on how to satisfy your lust and commit this sin with secrecy, but not at all to resist it; and this is a sign of a very unmortified heart.

Third, when men never vent and put forth their strength in prayer against those corruptions to which they are most subject, and are assaulted with one sin one day and another lust another day, and yet never go to God by prayer to beg for strength and mortifying grace to resist and keep under these corruptions, this is a sign of an unmortified heart. In Psalm 51:15 David says, "O Lord, open Thou my lips." One observed from this that as long as David lay under the guilt of his sin, all that time his mouth was shut; he could not pray to God. Therefore, after he had confessed his sin, he begged God to open his lips so that he might show forth His praise. As long as your mouth is shut so that you cannot pray against your corruptions, it is a sign that sin is not yet mortified in you.

Fourth, when corruptions and temptations to such and such sins most trouble and disturb you in holy duties; when a man is in an ordinance, and a lust shall tempt him there and fill his heart full of wickedness and worldly-mindedness; when sin and corruption so seize your heart that you cannot tell what a minister says in a whole hour—this argues that you have a very unmortified heart. In Jeremiah 23:11 God says, "In My house have I found their wickedness." When you give way to sinful thoughts and covetous imaginations in God's house, in the midst of holy duties, this discovers not only an unmortified, but a very impudent heart. The devil ravishes and deflowers you even in God's presence. Many young men come to church to look after and gaze upon handsome women, to cherish their lusts and speculative wantonness. Take heed of this, for it is an argument that you live after the flesh when you give way to such sinful temptations in holy duties when you should be attending God in His ordinances.

Fifth, it is an argument that sin is unmortified in your heart when calling to remembrance your former sinfulness does not humble you, but rather stirs up your corruptions afresh in your heart to plot and contrive how to commit the same sins again. It may be that you have been a drunkard in former times, and now you call to mind this sin with delight and study how to be drunk again; or perhaps you were an old fornicator or adulterer, and now you remember it and contrive how to commit this sin again. This is a sign of an unmortified heart. Ezekiel 23:21: "Thus thou calledst to remembrance the lewdness of thy youth, in bruising thy teats by the Egyptians for the paps of thy youth." The children of Israel, by calling to remembrance their adulteries in Egypt, fell again to their sinful pleasures.

Sixth, when a temptation to sin is quickly and easily closed with; when you can commit a great sin upon a small temptation; when your heart is like gunpowder to sin's touch, and it responds as did the young man whom the harlot met—in Proverbs 7:22 it is said, "He goeth after her straightway"—this is a sign of an unmortified heart.

Thus I have given you six characters, before the committing of sin, of an unmortified heart. There are three characters more that I shall lay down of an unmortified heart *after* the commission of any sin.

CHARACTER 1. This is when you find more joy in the pleasure of sin after the commission of it than you do sorrow for committing it; when you have more joy in regard to the sweetness of sin than you have sorrow in the consideration of the evil of sin.

CHARACTER 2. When you cannot endure a reproof for any sin you have committed, this argues an unmortified heart. When men are like nettles, that if you touch them ever so little they will sting you, so when you are told of your drunkenness or uncleanness or the like, you cannot let it go, but rage, brawl, and wrangle, this shows that you are asleep and dead in sin. When you cannot endure a reproof, nor abide to be awakened out of it; when you cannot abide it should be spoken against, it is a sign that you love sin well. James 1:19: "Let every man be swift to hear, slow to speak, slow to wrath." When the Word of God reproves you for a sin, you should be slow to wrath, not apt to be enraged at every reproof, but to "receive with meekness the engrafted Word that is able to save your souls," verse 21. An unmortified heart is very ready to storm and fume and fret when he is reproved.

CHARACTER 3. When you take more care, after the committing of a sin, to keep it secret from the view and knowledge of men than to repent and be humbled for it in the presence of God; when you labor rather to hide it than repent of it—this proceeds from the predominance of sin and corruption in your heart.

And thus I have given you nine discoveries of an unmortified heart. The Lord give you all grace to seriously inquire into your own souls whether you are mortified men and women or not.

USE OF REPROOF. The use that I shall make of this shall be of reproof. If it is so that those who live after the flesh shall die, then how blameworthy are all of you who incur this dismal judgment of eternal death; who rather than kill your sins let sin kill your soul. It is reported of the basilisk that if you do not kill him he will kill you. So it is here: if you do not kill your sins, your sins will be the death of your soul. Therefore, how blameworthy are you who would rather suffer sin to kill your souls than take any pains to mortify and subdue your sins!

I have read of a man who loved a fox so much that, notwithstanding that the fox had pulled out the bowels of one of his children, he would not part with it. I fear there are many of you who harbor such ravenous lusts and corruptions in your hearts that will destroy your souls. Yet you will not part with them, but suffer them to rule and reign in you, never going to God by prayer to beg for mortifying grace to subdue and keep them under.

Thus I am done with the first branch of the text: "If you live after the flesh, you shall die."

Sermon 2

"But if ye through the Spirit do mortify the deeds of the body, ye shall live." Romans 8:13

The Necessity of Mortification

I now come to the second part of the verse: "But if ye through the Spirit do mortify the deeds of the body, ye shall live."

Mortifying the deeds of the body cannot be understood of the religious deeds of the body, for they are to be cherished, nor of the natural deeds of the body such as eating and drinking; but it refers to the sinful actions that are done by the body arising from the temptations and injections of Satan, or the corrupt dictates of our own sinful nature.

"But if ye through the Spirit do mortify the deeds of the body, ye shall live." You see here, beloved, that the Lord walks in ways contrary to the judgments of flesh and blood. He bids us mourn and sow in tears and then we shall reap in joy. He bids us die, and tells us this is the way to live; and no way can be more contrary to flesh and blood, and yet there is no other way to live but this. We must first die to sin and the world before we can live a life of grace; and we must die a natural death before we can come to live a life of glory.

There are two observations that I shall draw from this latter part of the text:

DOCTRINE 1. Mortification of corruption is a necessary qualification required in every person who shall obtain salvation.

If you mortify the deeds of the body, you shall live.

DOCTRINE 2. From the addition of this phrase, "through the Spirit," observe that, though a man can commit sin by his own strength, he cannot mortify sin but by the strength of the Spirit.

These are the two points I intended to insist upon from the latter part of the text. I shall, by God's assistance, speak to the first of them in several sermons, but shall only at this time lay down something by way of introduction to this needful doctrine of mortification. Then I shall come to handle those things that are most useful and necessary to be known about this doctrine. I shall give you the nature and characters of it, the false mistakes about it, and the jealousies of godly people whereby they think they are not mortified when they are. At present I shall only speak something introductory to the clearer handling of the point that mortification of corruption is a necessary qualification required in every person who would attain to salvation.

First I shall lay down nine rules to those who are unmortified, then so many more to such as are mortified. I shall begin with the first, to those who are unmortified.

RULE 1. Count not the restraining of sin from coming into action to be a real mortifying of sin. Restraining grace is not mortifying grace. In Genesis 20:6 God said to Abimelech, "I withheld thee from sinning against Me; therefore suffered I thee not to touch her." He had sin restrained, but not mortified.

A lion confined within the grates is a lion still, though he cannot go about to devour his prey; similarly, though men are restrained from acting out those sins to which they are inclined, yet the restraint of sin is not to be taken for the mortifying of sin. A man may for a time lay a curb and restraint upon his lusts, so that they do not come forth into action, even without the powers of mortifying grace. A man may bridle a lust for many years, and yet the lust remains unmortified. Therefore, I say, do not count the restraining of a sin to be the mortifying of a sin.

RULE 2. A listlessness toward any kind of sin is no infallible demonstration that such a sin is mortified. Count not a present listlessness to some sins to be a saving mortification of them. This is a great mistake that many men run into: because they have no desire to commit some sins which their education makes them averse to, therefore they think they have a work of mortification and sanctification wrought in them; whereas there are divers external causes that may make a man indisposed and averse to some sins such as sickness, old age, horror of conscience, education, or a man's own natural temper. These causes are expounded in answer to the following question.

QUESTION. Why are men more disposed to some sins than others?

ANSWER 1. A man may have a listlessness and unwillingness toward some sins arising from a fit of sickness, so that, though he has been a drunkard or an adulterer in former times, yet because he has thereby distempered himself and impaired his health he has no lust or desire for those sins now. Or, if he has renewed desires after those sins, yet it may be that he wants strength of body to act. Such listlessness to sin, flowing from a sick bed, does not proceed from mortifying grace.

ANSWER 2. This indisposition to sin may flow from old age, wherein a man's strength is wasted and decayed, and so he is not able to commit those sins of adultery and drunkenness which formerly he committed and took pleasure in.

ANSWER 3. It may flow from a good education and principles of morality in men which restrain them from many gross and scandalous sins.

ANSWER 4. It may proceed likewise from horror and terror of conscience. When this seizes upon a man in whose face God casts the flashes of hellfire, this may make him abstain from sin for a time while the horror lies upon him. As a thundering storm sours the beer in our cellars, so, when God thunders upon the conscience, it will sour and embitter sin to a man so that he has no desires after it for the present. Yet this is not mortifying grace upon the heart, but the horror of conscience that gnaws and grips and terrifies the man, and makes him listless after sin at such a time.

ANSWER 5. Another external cause of a man's listlessness to some sins may be his natural temper. For, though every man has sin in him seminally, yet there are some sins which by nature he is more inclined to than others, according to his constitution. A man of a choleric disposition is most inclined to anger; a man of a sanguine disposition is most inclined to uncleanness. There are many sins that, by a man's natural temper, he is most averse to. Luther professed of himself that he was never in all his lifetime troubled with covetousness. This did not proceed from mortifying grace, but from the natural temper of his body. It was a gift of nature given him by God, and not a gift of grace.

Give me leave to illustrate this to you by this familiar similitude. Suppose you put a dog and a sheep together, and cast flesh before the sheep and grass before the dog. Neither of them will eat anything. The sheep will not eat the flesh; neither will the dog eat grass, which arises from the natural temper of the creatures. Why, so it is here. Men's natural tempers dispose them to some sins and not to others, which therefore is not to be imputed to the power of mortifying grace.

Therefore, beloved, you are not to impute to mortifying grace what is merely the result of a violent sickness, old age, education, terrors of conscience, or a man's natural temper and constitution.

RULE 3. Let mortification be extended to inward and secret sins as well as to outward and scandalous sins. Not only the lusts of the flesh, but those of the mind are to be mortified; not only the deeds of the body, but the thoughts of the heart and corruptions in the inward man are to be subdued. You are to extend mortification to the subduing of vicious affections as well as base actions. In Colossians 3:5 the Apostle says, "Mortify, therefore, your members which are upon the earth, fornication, uncleanness," and so on. You think, it may be, that these two are one. No, fornication is sin in action; uncleanness is sinning in affection and thought. The Apostle bids them mortify fornication, that is, uncleanness in action; but he does not stop there. He tells them they must subdue their sinful affections and vicious inclinations to those sins. You must mortify the very first motions and secret propensities to any sin in your hearts.

RULE 4. Let mortification be especially directed to strike at those sins that are your master sins—that are most prevalent and predominant in your heart, that you have most prayed against and are least able to resist, that strongly assault you and most easily beset you and are master over you. Thus David, in Psalm 18:23, says, "I have kept myself from mine iniquity," that is, from my special sins, my constitutional sins, my bosom iniquities. I might give you the same advice that the King of Syria gave his captains in 2 Chronicles 18:30: "Fight neither with small nor great, but only with the King of Israel." So I say to you, fight not so much against any sin as against your beloved, darling, constitutional sins that most easily beset you and prevail over you.

RULE 5. Think not to compass this great work of mortification by a general, superficial sight of sin, unless you come to a distinct and particular apprehension of your sins. If you take your sins and corruptions all together in a lump, you will never be able to break and mortify them. When a bundle of rods is knit closely one to another, the strongest man in the world is not able to break them; yet, if they are taken asunder, any man may break them all one by one with ease. So it is here: if you take sin apart and labor to have a distinct view and sight of each one, this is the way to overcome and mortify sin. If you shoot at random, you will never hit the mark. So, if you look at sins in general, in the lump, you will never be able to mortify them. If a man were enjoined to carry a great tree a good distance from his house, the way to do it is not to draw the whole body of the tree together, for this would be impossible; but he must cut the tree in pieces, and then he may easily do it. Similarly, many men go about to subdue and beat down sin in their hearts, but they think to do it all at once—and this is not the way. You must labor to take sin in pieces, to have a particular view of each one, to break and master them one by one; and thereby you shall be able to overcome the strongest of them.

RULE 6. Let your mortification extend not only to particular acts of sin, but to the whole bulk and body of sin. It is a great fault among many Christians that if they are troubled with passions, they go about to mortify them while forgetting their other sins. Or, if they are troubled with unclean and sinful thoughts, they endeavor to subdue them, yet, in the meantime, they leave the whole body of sin unmortified. In contrast, whenever you go about to mortify any one particular lust, you should labor to bewail the whole body of sin that is in you and to strike at the very root of sin. When a man would keep a tree from growing, he must not only lop off the branches, for that will not do it, but he must pluck it up by the root. So you may cut off one sin after another and make those branches wither, but if you do not pull up sin by the root, the other sins will but make your corruptions rage all the more. If not the same sins, yet others will appear, and perhaps sins worse than the former will grow up in place of them. When David bewailed his sin of adultery, he likewise bewailed the sin of his nature. In Psalm 51:5 he said, "Behold, I was shapen in iniquity and in sin did my mother conceive me," to show that when we go about to mortify any one particular sin we must likewise bewail and labor to bring under the whole body of sin.

RULE 7. When you are setting upon the work of mortification, go about it in the strength of Christ and not in your own strength. I told you before, you may commit sin by your own strength, but you cannot mortify sin by your own strength. "If ye through the Spirit do mortify the deeds of the body, ye shall live." Only an arrow fetched from Christ's quiver can slay your lusts. Therefore, do not depend upon your own reason, understanding, or knowledge in managing this great work of mortification and grappling with sin. For, though you may discover your sin, and your danger by reason of it, yet by your own strength you are not able to subdue and overcome that sin. "We are kept by the power of God unto salvation" (1 Peter 1:5).

Do not encounter sin with confidence in your own strength, for you are but a feather before a whirlwind. You have no power of your own to resist the weakest temptation or subdue the least corruption. Therefore, do as David did when he was to encounter Goliath, a great and mighty giant, and himself but a poor little stripling. What did David do? He said in 1 Samuel 17:45: "Thou comest to me with a sword and with a spear and with a shield; but I come against thee in the name of the Lord of hosts, and in the power of His might." So if you go out against your sins in the power of God's might, this is the only way to subdue them and keep under your unruly lusts.

RULE 8. Take heed of suffering sin to remain long in your heart without control, but labor to mortify it in its very first motions. When your nature first begins to close with a sin, then labor to root it out; for it's easier to keep sin out of our souls than it is to drive out sin once it has gotten into our hearts. Sin is like a serpent, which, if he can but get his head into any place, he will soon wind in his whole body. If we cherish and give entertainment to the first motions and inclinations of sin, it will quickly insinuate itself unto us. Sin is like the overflowing of a mighty river: once the water has made a breach in the bank, if it is not presently stopped, it will soon overflow the whole meadow. If we let sin alone in its first motions, it will quickly overrun the whole man.

RULE 9. When you have, through the strength of Christ, mortified one sin or resisted one temptation, do not sit down and think your work is done, but expect another combat. Your corruption will come afresh upon you again. The devil will still be plotting against you, and sending one temptation after another to foil you if he can. God suffers him to do this in a great deal of wisdom, to try us and humble us and let us see what continual cause we have of standing upon our guard and keeping a constant watch over our own hearts. As long as we live we shall stand in need of mortifying grace. Just as the branches of a tree, though you lop them off, will spring out again, so, when you have mortified one corruption, another will spring forth. Though you have cut off one lust today, it may be that another will spring out tomorrow. If you have mortified pride today, passion, covetousness or worldly-mindedness may spring up tomorrow; so we have continual cause of standing upon our watchtower and observing these deceitful hearts of ours which are always in need of mortifying grace to keep under our corruptions.

Thus I have done with these nine rules of caution touching this doctrine of mortification, which will all be very useful in handling many points that I shall treat upon in this subject. And because in what I have already said, it may be, I have been near the bosoms of many of you and touched your souls to the quick, there may be some poor, humble soul among you who has the power of mortifying grace upon his heart, and yet is ready to despond because he finds his corruptions to be so stirring and active in him that he is not able to master them. Therefore, will you follow me in your thoughts a little while I lay down seven comforting considerations in this particular?

CONSIDERATION 1. The stirring and rising of corruptions in the heart may yet be consistent with true mortification. The very lust that is mortified may yet make a great deal of stir and rising in the soul. And this consideration would administer a great deal of comfort to many poor souls were they but satisfied in this particular. In Romans 7:9 Paul says, "When the commandment came, sin revived." Yet Paul was a mortified and a sanctified man. It is with a godly man as with a man sick from a violent fever: though the man may be very near death, the strength of the disease may be so powerful upon him as to make him toss and tumble, so that two or three men shall scarcely be able to hold him quiet in his bed; yet this cannot be imputed to the strength of the man, but to the strength of the disease making him do this. So it may be in many a poor soul: sin may be very near its death, and mortification may yet stir and rage more than ever. This proceeds not from the weakness of the man to resist sin, but from the strength of Satan's temptations. It is the same with many birds: after their heads are pulled off they flutter more strongly than ever before. So you may give a mortal wound to a sin and yet, when the head (as it were) of sin is off, it may keep a great deal of stir in your soul.

But here, beloved, because I know there may be a great deal of ill use made of this comforting consideration, let me tell you that in two cases the stirring of corruptions and their workings in your soul do not argue an unmortified heart.

The first case is that in which, when corruptions stir in you, so your resolutions and striving against these sins and humiliation for them stir in you too. When the suggestions of Satan and solicitations to sin increase, your hearty prayers to God and resolutions against those sins increase too. When you can neither be quiet for sin, nor sin be quiet for you, in this case the stirring of corruptions does not argue an unmortified heart, but rather that sin already has received its death blow.

Second, the stirring of corruptions in your heart, though they are very violent, does not argue that your heart is unmortified, if after such turbulent stirring and struggling of sin in your heart these corruptions grow weaker and weaker. It is with sin in a godly man as it is with men in hot diseases that distemper the brain when a violent fit comes upon them: it makes them so outrageous and unruly that a man would admire how a poor, lean, sickly man should be so strong. But when the fit is over and the strength of the disease passes, the poor man, by his former struggling, is a great deal more faint, feeble, and weak. If it is thus with you, and if your struggling with sin becomes the weakening of sin so that, when corruptions have stirred in you, you have stirred against them and overcome them, and you find their strength abated and decayed, this is a very great evidence and argument of mortifying grace in your heart.

CONSIDERATION 2. Consider that mortification of sin does not reach so far in any regenerate man as to the utter abolition and extirpation of sin out of the soul. Never expect that it should extend this far. It is with sin in the soul as it was with the plague of leprosy in some cases: if the plague had spread in the walls of the house and was a fretting leprosy, it could not be gotten out by scraping or washing, but the house must be pulled down and demolished. So the leprosy of sin will cleave to you as long as you live in this world, until this body of yours is dissolved.

I compare sin in the soul to the tree you read of in Daniel 4:14–15, whose branches were cut off but yet the stump and root still remained. So you may lop off the branches of sin, but you can never quite eradicate and pluck it up by the roots. Do what you can, sin will vex you and disturb you as long as you live in this world. Therefore, I say, do not expect that mortification should extend so far as to a total abolition and utter extirpation of sin.

CONSIDERATION 3. Take this for your comfort: though God never intended that mortification should reach so far as to the utter extirpation of sin, God does intend that it should reach so far as to the taking away of the domination of sin. Though it does not take away the existence of sin, it does take away the dominion and reigning power of sin. It shall be in your souls as with those beasts spoken of in Daniel 7:12: "Their dominion shall be taken away but their lives shall be prolonged for a little season."

So God will permit sin to live in you for a little season, but not to reign in you. Romans 6:14: "Sin shall not have dominion over you for you are not under the law, but under grace." You are under neither the rigor nor the power of the law; therefore, sin shall not have dominion over you because you are not under the law but under grace. You are not under sin as a law, but under the command and law of grace (for "the law" is there to be interpreted as the law of sin). In Romans 7:23 it is the Apostle's dialect to call sin by the name of a law: "I see a law in my members warring against the law of my mind." Sin shall not have dominion over you, though its life and existence are prolonged for a little season.

CONSIDERATION 4. Take this for your comfort: an expulsive faculty or a sincere endeavor by the soul to expel and mortify sin is accepted by God as real mortification. If the Lord sees you stand, as it were, in battle array against your lusts, and sees that you grapple with every sin and resist every temptation, and sees that you stand your guard with your weapons in your hand, God looks upon this principle of resistance as if it were a perfect resistance.

There is a notable passage in Leviticus 11:33–36, where you read that it was a part of the ceremonial law that if any unclean thing fell into a vessel of water, both the water and the vessel were unclean; but if it fell into a spring or fountain of water it was not unclean. Interpreters give this reason for it: if any unclean thing fell into a vessel of water, which has no purging faculty to cleanse itself, it must be unclean; but if any unclean thing fell into a fountain or river of water it was not defiled because, by its continual gliding motion, the water cleansed itself from all filthiness that fell into it. So here, if you have no principle at all within you that stirs you up to resist and withstand your corruption, to cleanse and root sin out of your heart, you are then unclean. But if, when sin falls upon you, by a holy industry and continual striving against sin from a principle of grace within you, labor to cleanse and purge and free yourself from those sins, in this case you are not to be pronounced an unclean and unmortified man. Oh, what unspeakable comfort may this afford every one of you, that your resisting and encountering sin is looked upon by God as a total subduing and overcoming of it!

CONSIDERATION 5. Another comforting consideration is this: consider that you have God's promise and Christ's power to help you in managing this great work of mortification. Beloved, there is never a mother's child among you belonging to Christ who encounters and fights with the devil alone or bears his own burdens alone. There are none of you who have an interest in Christ but have God's promise and Christ's power to help and assist you in the mortifying of every sin. Therefore, it is observable that in some places God commands us to mortify sin. Colossians 3:5: "Mortify, therefore, your members which are upon the earth, (such as) fornication, uncleanness."

In other places God has promised to do it Himself for us. Micah 7:19: "He will subdue our iniquities." As God commands His children to obey Him, so He conveys power and ability to enable them to do what He commands. God bids them mortify sin.

"Alas," says a poor soul, "I am not able to grapple with my corruptions and to keep them under."

"Why, then," says God, "I will help you and subdue and mortify sin for you."

Oh, what a gracious Captain we fight under who does our work for us and yet gives us the honor of it, who fights our battles for us and yet gives us the glory of the victory! Oh, what a comfort this is, that we have such a good God to fight for us and subdue our iniquities for us!

CONSIDERATION 6. Sin and corruption may be more stirring and boisterous after a man is regenerate than they were before conversion. Thus it was with Paul in Romans 7:9: "I was alive without the law once, but when the commandment came, sin revived and I died." It is as if he had said, "Before I was converted, I was alive; no sin at all troubled me. I thought myself in a very good and happy condition. I was a blameless man, but when the commandment came, sin revived."

When the commands of God came, which means

the Ten Commandments, they limited our very thoughts, so that we must not have so much as a sinful or covetous thought. If we do, this sin alone would be enough to condemn us, even if we were blameless in regard to all the other commandments. "When this commandment came, then sin revived and I died," that is, I saw myself in a lost and undone condition without a Savior. Now these stirrings of sin after conversion do not argue that there is more sin in the soul than there was before conversion, but only that it is more discovered and obvious to a man, so that he sees himself as sinful beyond measure. You did not have so quick an eye to discern sin before as you now have.

I might illustrate this to you by this similitude. Suppose any of you were knocking or striking your finger against a stool or chair or any such thing, and all of a sudden, by accident, should cut it. Now the least knock or touch of your finger after it is cut will make it smart. You might have knocked it again and again before and yet never felt it, whereas now everything that touches it troubles you.

So it is with a man after conversion. The poor man cries out, "Lord, what is the matter that this sin and that sin trouble me? It was not that way before." The reason is that your conscience was not as tender before conversion as now it is. You could not then discern the small and lesser sins as you can now when the Lord Jesus Christ radiates and shines forth with His bright beams upon your soul, enlightening it and uncovering the secret sins that lie lurking there.

CONSIDERATION 7. Last, take this for your comfort: in your endeavors to mortify sin, you may die by yielding to sin, but you shall never die by opposing and resisting sin. It is not good to cry for quarter at sin's hands. You can never die by grappling with sin, but you may die by yielding to sin. Those sins shall never damn you that you have labored and prayed against and encountered. But if you, like a faint-hearted soldier, run away and yield to Satan's temptations and assaults, then you are undone. You may be damned by yielding to sin, but you shall never be damned by fighting against sin; therefore, labor and earnestly beg God to give you the power of mortifying grace in your hearts that you may be enabled to mortify and keep under sin and bring the flesh to be subject to the spirit. Thus, I have given you in all sixteen rules as an introduction to this great doctrine of mortification.

Sermon 3

"But if ye through the Spirit do mortify the deeds of the body, ye shall live." Romans 8:13

Several Questions about Mortification

I shall now fall upon the discussion of several queries about this doctrine.

1. I shall show you the nature of mortification.

2. I shall show you the necessity of it in reference to salvation.

3. I shall show you the discoveries whereby you may know whether God has brought you into a state of mortification or not.

4. I shall show the great mistakes that many men fall into about this doctrine of mortification. Some think they are mortified when they are not; others think they are not mortified when indeed they are.

5. I shall show you the great difficulty of this duty, and divers other necessary things touching this doctrine. I shall dispatch three of these queries at present, but I intend to insist more largely on the latter.

QUESTION 1. What is the nature of mortification?

ANSWER. I shall give you this plain description of it: It is a holy disposition in a regenerate man derived from the efficacy and virtue of Christ's death, whereby the strength of sin is weakened and the dominion of it destroyed, being utterly disabled from having a commanding power or rule over the man any more.

I say it is a disposition in a *regenerate* man because an unregenerate man is an unmortified man. It is derived from the virtue and efficacy of Christ's death because the death of Christ not only takes away the guilt of sin, in reference to its damning power, but it likewise takes away the dominion and power of sin so that sin shall not reign in us. And I express it further as the disposition whereby the strength of sin is weakened and the dominion and power of it destroyed; not that I extend mortification to an utter abolition and extirpation of sin, but only to the subduing and weakening of our corruptions. Though the existence of sin remains, yet the commanding power of sin is taken away.

QUESTION 2. What is the necessity of this great work of mortification?

ANSWER. It lies in three things:

1. It is very necessary by way of evidence to know whether you belong to Christ or not. There is nothing in the world that will more truly evidence your having an interest in God than this: the Lord has brought you into a state of mortification. You can have no interest in a living God if there are still living lusts and corruptions remaining in you.

I might make use of a story I have sometimes told you of an island that lies between Scotland and Ireland. There was a controversy between the two nations as to which of them the island belonged to. The matter was decided in this way: they took a great many toads, serpents, and unclean creatures and put them on the island. If these unclean and venomous beasts lived, the island belonged to Scotland; but if they died then it must belong to Ireland, because no unclean beasts can live there. I make this application of it: there is a great controversy between God and the devil concerning to whom your soul belongs. If venomous lusts and unclean corruptions live in your heart, and rule and reign there, this is an argument that you belong to Satan; but if sin does not live or reign in you, this is an undeniable argument that you belong to God.

2. The necessity of mortification also consists in this: since grace cannot live in your soul unless sin and corruption are dead, before there can be the life of grace there must be the death of sin. Romans 6:11: "Reckon yourselves to be dead indeed unto sin, but alive unto God." If corruptions live, grace cannot live in your heart. It is reported that doves cannot live in smoky and nasty places; so the Spirit of God will not live in that soul which is full of nasty corners of sin and corruption.

3. Finally, the necessity of mortification appears in this: the soul cannot live in glory till sin dies in the heart. As grace cannot live in the heart till sin is subdued, neither can the soul live in glory hereafter till sin is dead and mortified. As one well says, "If sin does not die, the sinner must die." If God does not kill your sins, sin will kill your soul. The Apostle says in 1 Corinthians 15:36: "Thou fool, that which thou sowest is not quickened, except it die." As the grain dies and rots in the ground before it is quickened and springs up again, so your soul cannot be quick-

ened and made capable of living with God in glory till your corruptions are rotten, dead, and destroyed in your soul. This much shall suffice touching the necessity of mortification.

QUESTION 3. How may I know whether the Lord has brought me into a state of mortification or not? I shall be somewhat longer in this query. It may be that some of you are very desirous to be satisfied in it, so I shall give you six revealing characteristics of it and go over them very briefly.

1. Would you know whether God has brought you into a state of mortification or not? You may know it by this characteristic: if you are now more fearful of running into occasions and opportunities of sin than you have been in times past, this is an argument that you are a mortified man. An unmortified heart is bold and venturous and will rush upon occasions of sin, whereas a mortified heart is very careful to avoid all occasions of evil.

One compares a mortified man to a dove or partridge. Now such as use that game of hawking report that such an innate fear and dread doves or partridges have of the hawk that they not only fear the hawk but the very feathers of it. So a mortified man not only fears a downright sin, but also anything that may be a provocation or inlet to a sin. Now if this holy fear of displeasing and offending God is found in you, I may safely pass this sure judgment upon you: you are a mortified man when you are in such a gracious frame and temper of spirit as that in Jude 23, when you hate the garment spotted with the flesh. It is a metaphoric expression, alluding to those who had the plague of leprosy under the law in Leviticus 13:45. The children of Israel not only feared touching such a man, but they would not touch his garment or come near his house or anything he had. So we should hate the garment spotted with the flesh, that is, avoid everything that may threaten infection or occasion a sin.

2. Another discovery is this: when an occasion of committing a sin is openly offered to a man, along with concurring circumstances that might provoke him to that sin, yet he will restrain and bridle his appetite and will not commit that sin. This is a sign of a truly mortified heart, and if God has brought you into such a frame He has thoroughly mortified your corruptions.

Beloved, an unmortified man may abstain from a sin when there is no opportunity or occasion offered to commit that sin. But this is an argument of a mortified heart: though all occasions for acting a sin concur, yet he will abstain from it. You have instances of two men who discovered their mortification in this regard. One of them was Joseph in Genesis 39:9. He had a fair occasion offered him to commit the sin of adultery. He had opportunity, for he and his mistress were alone, and he had importunity, for she urged and solicited him from day to day to do it. He had secrecy, too, for the text says that the doors were shut. There was none but the two of them in the house. He might have gotten a great deal of preferment and advantage by it, for she would have made him lord over her house. You see that here was opportunity, importunity, secrecy, and advantage. All these occasions were clearly offered and concurred to invite Joseph to the sin of uncleanness. Yet, for all this, Joseph replied: "How shall I do this great wickedness and so sin against God?" Here you see the power of sin mortified in Joseph's heart. Now, do you try your own hearts by this pattern, that when all occasions are offered for committing a sin, you can still say "no" to your lusts?

Another instance is David in 1 Samuel 24:4. Saul came into the same cave where David and his men lay, and the text says that while Saul was in the cave David came and cut off the lap of his robe privately. Now David might just as easily have cut off his head if he would. Though Saul pursued David to take away his life, when David had an opportunity to cut off Saul's head he would not do it, and this evidenced the sin of revenge mortified in David's heart. Now, I beseech you, examine your hearts in these two particulars and see how the case stands between God and your own souls.

3. If there is any tendency in your heart toward a greater resistance against the devil's temptations to sin than formerly, this is a good argument that the Lord has brought you into a state of mortification. It may be that heretofore your nature was like gunpowder, apt to be in a flame upon any temptation. But now it is like green wood that will lie a great while upon the fire before it burns. So a temptation can hardly persuade you to yield to it. If it is thus with you, you have made great progress in this work of mortification.

4. If there is a fair proportion between the death of sin and the life of grace in your soul, then you are a mortified man. Beloved, the Lord's work is not a

half work, to kill corruptions in your heart and no more; but if the Lord has savingly subdued sin in your soul, He will work a contrary work of grace in you that shall live and act in your soul. Mortification and the death of sin must come in tandem with vivification and the life of grace. So if sin is dead, grace shall live in your soul; and therefore, the Apostle joins them both together in Romans 6:11: "Reckon yourselves dead unto sin, but alive unto God." 1 Peter 4:1–2: "For he that hath suffered in the flesh hath ceased from sin, that he no longer should live the rest of his time in the flesh to the lusts of men but to the will of God." Here the Apostle not only enjoins us not to spend our time in fulfilling the lusts of the flesh, but to live unto God. Therefore, beloved, that is only a cessation, not a mortification of corruption, where there is a forcible restraint laid upon your lusts. They only *seem* to be dead, but are not so really.

5. Mortification is discovered by this characteristic: where the keeping under of any corruption is the result of a deep humiliation. The mortification that never had true humiliation preceding it is but a mere cessation from sin. Your sins have never yet been truly mortified if your heart has not been truly humbled. Many men do with their sins as fencers do upon a stage: sometimes they give one another a slight blow or scare, but they never strike a deadly stroke. Some men will play with sin, but never give it a mortal wound. A truly mortified man is like a warrior: he will either kill or be killed. He will kill his sins or else his sin will kill him. Now examine yourselves in this: are you only fencers, to sport and play

with your lusts, or are you warriors who fight with an implacable opposition against sin? Do you only give a slight scare to sin or have you given it a deadly wound?

6. Mortification may be discovered by its breadth, for it does not consist in the killing of any one particular sin, but in striking at the root and whole body of sin. And therefore, the Apostle exhorts us to mortify our members which are on the earth—fornication, uncleanness, etc.—and to crucify the flesh with its affections and lusts; to keep under the whole body of sin. It is with the mortification of sin as it is with the dying of the body. You know that death is not a seizure upon the arm or leg, or any one or two members, but upon all the members of the body—all must die. So mortification is not the killing of any one member of sin, but a seizure upon the whole body of sin. The keeping under of some particular sins does not argue mortification unless you have given a mortal wound to the very body and bulk of corruption.

USES. And thus I am done with the doctrinal part of these three questions. I shall now speak by way of application before I come to handle the other questions, about which I shall spend a great deal more time. But for the present, the use that I shall make of what I have already delivered shall be this: It may be that this doctrine may unsettle many a conscientious heart, and many a godly man may pass a very hard censure upon his own heart. I think that sin is yet alive in his soul and grace dead. Therefore, I have seven comforting words to lay down to such as you are. Then, if time will permit, I shall proceed to the handling of other questions.

USE 1. The first comforting word I have to say to those who complain that their corruptions are unmortified is this: there may be a mortification of corruption in that heart where there is a strong irritation of corruption. The devil may irritate, that is, he may strongly stir up corruptions in your heart, and yet you may be in a mortified state. I shall have occasion hereafter to speak more fully to this point, and therefore I shall only now add that passage previously quoted in Romans 7:9 where Paul says, "When the commandment came, sin revived and I died." Paul thought himself alive before and sin dead. He was, in his own apprehensions, according to the law blameless; but when the Lord gave Paul a spiritual insight into his own heart, then he perceived himself to die and sin to revive. So there may be a stirring up of sin in the heart, and yet those very sins have their death wound.

USE 2. Take this for your comfort: the reiteration and later committing of the same sin do not argue that your heart is void of mortification. I only name this to you because I intend to make a distinct question of this, whether a man who has a corruption truly mortified may fall often into the same sin.

USE 3. Take this for your comfort: the mortification of corruption was never intended by God to extend so far as to the total abolition and utter extirpation of sin, but if the domination of sin is destroyed the Lord looks upon it as mortification. Sin is (as I told you before) like that tree spoken of in Daniel, whose branches were cut off but the stump remained; so if the dominion and ruling power of sin is taken away, you are in a good enough condition.

Reverend Mr. Perkins uses a very clear similitude to explain this great work of mortification. He speaks of the husbandman who washes his corn never so clean before he sows it. Yet notwithstanding this, when it springs and grows up again it will not come up clean, but there will be chaff among it, and there will be a stalk and a blade and other things that pertain to the corn, though they were never sown with the corn. So, though you wash your heart never so clean from sin, some corruption will still spring up in your heart. God reserves the utter abolition of sin for the state of glorification, not of mortification.

USE 4. You who complain that your corruptions are unmortified, take this for your comfort: God will never expose you to more violent temptations to sin than what you shall be able to vanquish and overcome in the end. You may be sure to have no more laid upon you than you have strength to grapple with. What if temptations to sin are strong, as long as God gives a sufficiency of grace and strength to withstand and encounter them?

It is a very good observation which some make from Genesis 26:2 compared with Genesis 46:3, where we read that there were two great famines in the land wherein Isaac and Jacob lived. Now when there was a famine in the land in Isaac's days, he inquired of the Lord whether he should go down into Egypt to buy corn, and the Lord told him he should not. God denied Isaac permission to go down, but afterwards, when there was a famine in Jacob's days, he likewise asked of the Lord whether he should go down and God bade him go in Genesis 46:3. Now why did the Lord forbid Isaac and yet suffer Jacob to go down into Egypt? Commentators give a very good reason for it: God would not let Isaac go down because he was a weak believer. God said that he was a weak Christian, and was not able to grapple with temptation and withstand all the occasions and opportunities of sin he might meet with in Egypt; therefore, he was not to go. But Jacob was a strong believer, and able to encounter any temptation; therefore God bade him go. Here you see that the Lord will not lay upon His children more than they are able to bear. Oh, what a great comfort this should be to us, that we have so good a God to serve who carries such tender bowels towards all His children!

You have a passage to this purpose in Isaiah, showing that when you are weak and young converts, the Lord will stay His rough winds and will proportion the temptations according to your strength. Isaiah 28:27: "The fitches are not threshed with a threshing instrument, neither is a cart wheel turned about upon the cummin; but the fetches are beaten out with a staff and the cummin with a rod." As the smaller seeds, fitches and cummin, must not be beaten out with great weights but with a rod and a staff, so weak Christians shall not be exposed to great afflictions and temptations but such as are proportionate to their strength, and strong believers shall have temptations answerable to their strength. God will lay upon His children no more than they are able to bear.

USE 5. Know this for your comfort: in some cases strong temptation to sin is not a sin in the person tempted, but in the person tempting. A believer may think that if the devil dogs him from day to day and from place to place and from time to time, continually urging and soliciting him to wickedness, the Lord will charge all this upon him as his guilt. But if a temptation to sin were always a sin in the person tempted, then Christ Himself would have had sin in His nature (which would be blasphemy to say), for He was tempted by the devil to the two great sins of murder and covetousness. But these were not sins in the person tempted, but in the person tempting. So when you do not close with a temptation, but do what you can to resist and repel it; when sin does not arise from your own nature and inward corruptions, but merely of the devil's suggestion and instigation—these sins are none of yours, but shall be charged to the devil.

USE 6. Take this for your comfort: a principle of opposition, a principle of undaunted and irreconcilable opposition against every corruption, is accounted by God as mortification. Mortification on our part is but standing out against and doing battle with sin. And here I cannot but make use of that place previously quoted in Leviticus 11:33–36, where the Lord made a law that if any unclean thing fell into a vessel of water it would be unclean; but if it fell into a river of water it was not unclean. The reason is that a vessel of water has no purgative faculty to cleanse itself from any filthiness that falls into it, but a fountain or river of water, by its continual running, purges and cleanses itself from any unclean thing cast into it. So here, though corruptions are in your heart, yet, if you are like a running river, then you cleanse yourself from these sins, and the Lord looks upon you as a mortified man.

USE 7. Take this for your comfort: in the mortification of every sin, you have Christ's strength to help you as well as your own. Therefore, in some places He commands us to mortify sin; in other places, He promises to do it for us. Oh, what a good Master we serve, who does our work for us and yet pays us our wages! Though He Himself does all for us and we do nothing, yet He rewards us as if we had done it ourselves.

Sermon 4

"But if ye through the Spirit do mortify the deeds of the body, ye shall live." Romans 8:13

The Mistakes of Those Who Do Not Recognize Their Mortification

QUESTION 4. What are those mistakes that men run into about this great work of mortification?

ANSWER. There is a double mistake men are apt to fall into. There is a mistake on the right hand, which doubting and perplexed Christians run into when they conceive and are persuaded that their corruptions are not mortified when indeed they are. On the other hand, there is a mistake which presumptuous sinners run into whereby they imagine their corruptions are mortified when indeed they are not. I shall go through the first of these at this time, the mistake that doubting and perplexed Christians run into in concluding that their sins are not mortified when they are. In the pursuit of this, I shall show you three grand mistakes in the hearts of God's people that make them think their hearts are unmortified.

MISTAKE 1. "Oh," says a poor soul, "that which makes me think that my heart is not mortified is the strong motion and stirring of sin in my heart."

ANSWER. Now to correct this mistake, I have

only these seven words to say to you who make this a ground of your complaint that corruptions are not mortified because of the motions and stirring of sin in you:

1. Consider whether these motions to sin arise from the devil or from your own heart. And if these motions and instigations to sin proceed merely from the devil, from his malice and envy against your soul, then you have no cause to fear; for these stirrings and motions to sin in your soul argue that your sins are mortified. Christ Himself had strong motions and temptations to sin, and not small sins either, but sins of destruction and self-murder, to break His own neck and to a sin of covetousness. He was allured with the glory of the world.

Now, therefore, though you are often pestered and troubled by the devil, and followed at the heels by him with one temptation after another, if you can truly say these stirrings and motions to sin merely arise from Satan and do not proceed out of your own heart, if you can clear the case to be so, I will assure you that these are the devil's sins and not yours. The Lord will charge them upon his score and not yours. As we have noted, in some cases temptations to sin are not the corruptions of the person tempted, but of the devil tempting.

2. Suppose it is true that these motions and stirrings in your heart do not arise merely from Satan's injections, but from your own heart, which is like a sea that calls forth nothing but mire and dirt. Suppose your heart is like a cage for every unclean bird and a den for every unclean beast to lie down in. Suppose that the breathings of your heart are

like the reeking of dunghills that cast forth an evil and stinking savor. Yet if these motions are not yielded to with a ready and willing consent, but are resisted and opposed, these sins will never be damning sins to you. If your heart does not close with these sins, it is no argument that you are unmortified, but rather an evidence of the contrary. God will never damn you for that which you make the matter of your complaint, humiliation, and opposition. You may die running away from or yielding to the devil, but you shall never die fighting with him.

3. Take this for an answer: the stirrings and workings of corruption in your heart do not always argue that your corruptions have more strength and life in them than heretofore, but that you have more light to discover and discern them than formerly. St. Paul, before his conversion, thought himself according to the law blameless, but afterward, as he says in Romans 7:9: "When the commandment came, then sin revived and I died." Then he saw sin to have a greater power in his heart, not that he had more sin now than before, but because now he perceived it whereas before he did not.

A godly man who has a work of conversion newly wrought upon his heart, though he has a spiritual insight into his own heart, at first he only sees gross and outward evils, for it must be a very expert Christian who can discern inward and secret evils and smaller sins. Many men, after a long conversion, see more of the workings of sin in their hearts than ever they did discover before or at their first conversion. Now, such men have not an increase of sin, but an increase of illumination and light. On a gloomy day; though the air is very full of dust and small atoms, yet we cannot discern them; but if the sun shines, then you may see them clearly. They are there when the sun does not shine, though you cannot perceive them. This is the third answer: the motions and stirrings of sin in the heart do not always arise from the increase of strength and life in sin, but from the increase of light that God puts into the soul.

4. The stirrings of sin in your heart may not always argue the corruptions to be unmortified, but your conscience to be more tender than heretofore. Suppose you have a cut finger. When it is sore, anything that touches it troubles you; but before it was cut, you could knock your finger against anything and never take notice of it. It would neither smart nor trouble you. Now this does not argue that since you cut your finger you touch it more often against things that hurt it than before it was cut, but that now you are more sensitive and affected with every touch. So it is in this case: your conscience is now enlightened and you are more apprehensive and sensitive of the least sin than heretofore.

5. You are not to judge yourself to be unmortified by the stirring of corruption now and then, upon an extraordinary and violent temptation in your soul. Though a corruption is let loose upon you by some violent temptation sometimes, yet you are not to take an estimate of your mortification by this, but you are to judge yourself by the constant temper and ordinary frame of your heart. Is it ordinary with you for the heart to be like a cage of unclean birds, or like the sea continually casting forth mire and dirt?

If it is so, then you have cause to fear that sin is yet unmortified in your heart. If you were to give your judgments concerning the depth of a river, you are not to pass your verdict on its depth by its breadth after a great rain or cloud, but you are to judge by its ordinary course, running in its own channel. So you are not to judge the mortification of your corruptions by some extraordinary stirrings of sin in your soul after some violent temptation, but by the ordinary frame and temper of your heart.

6. Take this for your consolation: inward stirrings and workings of sin in your soul may in some cases argue more that sin is near its dissolution than that you are void of mortification, such as in these three cases:

First, if the workings of sin make you more watchful against all occasions of sin, and against the first motions of sin in your heart. As a wanton eye is a glance of a lustful heart, so a watchful eye is an evidence of a mortified heart.

Second, if the irritation of sin provokes you to humiliation for those sins, and to resolutions against them and strong supplications to God to enable you to subdue them, such a frame of heart argues strength of grace than strength of sin.

Third, if after such violent motions and stirring of sin in your soul, your corruptions grow weaker and feebler every day; this is a sign of your mortification of sin. The stirrings of lust, pride, or passion may be very great and unruly in your heart, and you may bemoan them and pray and strive against them and yet cannot keep them under; but if within a little while you perceive that these stirrings of sin have enfeebled it and make it decay in strength and grow weaker and weaker, in this case you have no need to fear that your sin is unmortified.

I told you before that the stirrings of sin in some men are like a dying man sick with a fever. When he is in the heat of his disease, and a violent fit comes upon him, the poor sick man will thrash and tumble, and three or four men shall scarcely be able to keep him in his bed. Now this doesn't proceed from the strength of the man, but from the strength of the disease. As soon as the fit is over, the man is so weak that there is scarcely life in him; he is not now able to stir or move himself. So when sin is in your soul like a burning fever upon a man, no exhortations, reproofs, or threatening can restrain or withhold you from sin, and from running after the fulfilling and satisfaction of the lusts and desires of your heart. Yet if you find that after these violent motions to sin your corruptions have been weakened and enfeebled, you have cause to bless God that He has begun this work of mortification in your heart, and has given Satan an irrecoverable blow.

7. Take this for your comfort: the stirrings of sin in your heart may be so ordered by God as to make them a means to engage you to a fuller mortification of your sins. Should not sin stir in your soul, but lie there still and quiet, you would be apt to grow secure and careless, and take no notice of the sinfulness of your heart. But when the stinking savor and noisome smell of your lusts rise up in your heart, this may be a means to encourage and quicken your endeavors to mortification, subduing, and rooting out of these corruptions within you.

Thus I am done with these seven particulars by way of comfort to those who complain that their hearts are unmortified because of the stirrings and motions to sin in their hearts.

MISTAKE 2. I now pass on to the second mistake which makes a godly soul fear that his heart is unmortified. "Oh," says another godly man, "I have not only the stirrings of sin in my heart, but the Lord has shown mercy to my soul. I am in a thousand times worse condition, for I find that I have prayed often, again and again, and bent all my endeavors against such a particular corruption, yet, notwithstanding all my prayers and endeavors, sighs and groans, that very sin has gotten ahead of me and prevailed over me, which could not mean but that sin is unmortified and has a great prevalence over my heart." I think I hear such breathings as these coming from a godly soul: "Oh, woe is me! I have made many a prayer and renewed many a purpose in my heart to keep out such a sin, but yet I cannot. Sin prevails and gets the victory over me, and I am not able to encounter it; therefore, this makes me fear whether I have the power of mortifying grace upon my heart."

ANSWER. Beloved, your condition is very sad; yet I have four words to say to you.

1. It may be that the evils you complain of, that you cannot keep under, are great and gross evils, but they are inward and unavoidable. If so, you have less cause for jealousy that your corruptions are unmortified. Indeed, if the sins you complain of are great and crying sins, then you have cause to fear; but if

they are only inward and unavoidable corruptions such as vain thoughts, distempered passions, spiritual pride, vainglory, or the like, you may make a thousand prayers against these and never be able to overcome them and root them out.

2. Suppose the corruptions are great that you have purposed and prayed against, and you cannot subdue them and bring them under. Yet know this for your comfort: this is as much as God requires of you—that you should resist and resolve against and labor to withstand your corruptions. If you do your duty in this, though you may be overcome, God will not hold you guilty. It is in this case as it was in the law that God made concerning a virgin in Deuteronomy 22:25–27. The law said that if a damsel was walking in the field alone, and a lustful man met her and laid with her, only the man who lay with her was to die; but they were not to meddle with the damsel, for he found her in the field, and the damsel cried, and there was none to help her.

Beloved, it is so in this case. It may be that the devil commits a spiritual rape upon you, and is so forcible with his temptation that you yield to him; but if before and after the commission of that sin you bewail it, hate it, detest it, and strive against it, the Lord will lay the sin on Satan's score, and require it of him and not of you.

3. You who complain that your corruptions are unmortified, who have prayed often against them and yet they are not subdued, take this for your comfort: your praying and purposing against sin is an undeniable argument that they are dying, though they are not quite dead. Were your corruptions liv-

ing, your heart would be dead, unfit and unable to pray. If your praying does not make you leave sinning, your sinning will make you leave praying. You who continually strive and pray against sin, it is an undoubted evidence that your corruptions are dying, though they are not dead. As some birds will flutter more strongly after their heads are pulled off than before, which is an undeniable argument that they are dying though not quite dead, so when you find such violent motions and stirrings of sin in you, notwithstanding all your prayers and endeavors to the contrary, yet you may be sure your corruptions are dying, though not yet dead.

4. Mark this for your comfort: corruption may have its deadly wound in general and yet a particular lust may be very vigorous and lively and active in your soul. It is a rule among divines that as all corruptions are not equally alive in a man, so neither are all corruptions equally dead in a man.

Here is your comfort: if you can prove that a general work of mortification is wrought in you, then the body of sin is destroyed. Though you have some particular corruptions yet remaining in you, this does not argue that you are unmortified. It is the same with a dying man: one of his limbs may die before another. His heart may have life when his leg or arm is dead, and if any one of his members is dead it argues that the man cannot live much longer. So if one sin is dead, it argues that the whole body of sin is mortified; though this or that particular lust prevails in your heart, yet the general work of mortification may be wrought in you, notwithstanding that some particular sins are not yet quite subdued.

MISTAKE 3. Another mistake that a godly man runs into is this: "Oh," says a poor soul, "it is true, I have cause to fear upon these two grounds already mentioned; but, alas, it is not only the stirrings of sin in my heart, and my frequent falling into sin after prayers and promises and resolutions against them, but that which especially makes me fear my corruptions are unmortified is that if corruptions were dying in me, I would find grace living and acting in me more than it does. Grace would hold an advanage over sin. As one decreases, the other would increase. Because I cannot find nor perceive grace to be vigorous and lively in my soul, it is, I fear, because sin is not yet dead in my heart."

ANSWER. To you who make this complaint, I have only three words to say for your comfort.

1. You must know that the whole work of grace and sanctification is not done at once. Indeed, you are justified at once, and elected at once, but you are not sanctified at once. You must not expect the whole work of sanctification to be wrought in a moment, but as a child comes to maturity and manhood, not presently but by degrees so the work of sanctification comes on slowly and by degrees.

2. Take this for your comfort: there may be a dying and decaying of common gifts when yet there may be a quick and lively acting of true and saving grace in your soul. It may be that you have lost that volubility of tongue, readiness of utterance, and strength of memory in your old age which you excelled at in your youth. These may become decayed even while grace grows in your soul.

A divine observed that though a musician can

play better upon an instrument in his younger days, and could sing more harmoniously and make a more pleasant melody than when he comes to be old, yet he has more skill and judgment in music now than he had before. So you may lose the varnish and flourish of your graces, and yet grow more in understanding, judgment, and experience now than ever you did before.

3. You who complain and fear that your corruptions are not dead because grace is not so lively and active in you, know this for your comfort: ordinarily God gives a greater amount of vivacity and quickness of grace at a man's first conversion than He gives ever after, because He wishes to allure men to religion and the practice of godliness.

Sermon 5

"But if ye through the Spirit do mortify the deeds of the body, ye shall live." Romans 8:13

The Mistakes of Those Who Think Their Corruptions Are Mortified When They Are Not

I come now to handle the mistakes on the other hand, those who think their corruptions are mortified when they are not. The heart of man is deceitful above all things, a bundle of deceit; and man himself is a proud creature, and very apt to have high conceits of himself. There are three grounds of mistakes in wicked men which make them think their corruptions are mortified when indeed they are not:

• Because they find an opposition against sin.

• Because they find in themselves the power of restraining grace.

• Because there is a leaving and forsaking of some sins in them. It may be that a man was an adulterer in former times, but he is not one now. Or he was a swearer or a drunkard in former times, but he is none of these now.

These are the three grounds of wicked men's mistakes in reference to this work of mortification. I shall spend two sermons answering these three mistakes, and showing you the weakness and insufficiency of these grounds to evidence a work of mortification upon their hearts.

GROUND 1. Because they find in themselves an opposition against some sins, they conclude that a work of mortification has taken place upon their hearts. I answer that an opposition to sin may proceed from the light of a natural conscience, which may convince a man what is sin and what is not. Even wicked men may have a law within them that makes them averse and opposed to some sins, such as uncleanness and drunkenness. Their consciences may accuse them when they do ill and excuse them when they do well, but only in general.

I shall now speak to it more particularly. I beseech you to lend me your thoughts a little, for I do not think there is a man or woman among you, though never so wretched and vile, but who has at one time or another withstood some corruptions and sinful motions in their hearts. I shall show eight particular cases wherein you may oppose corruptions and yet be an unmortified man. You may oppose them jestingly, sparingly, partially, hypocritically, slavishly, constrainedly, faintly, and politically.

First, a man may oppose corruptions jestingly. He may do as fencers used to do upon the stage when they pretended to hurt one another, but never gave a deadly wound. Though they may seem to hack and hew one another, they never draw one drop of blood, being in jest all the while. So though a wicked man opposes and resists sin, he will be sure not to hurt his sin. Now a mortified man opposes sin in earnest, and encounters it not as a fencer, but as a warrior opposes his mortal enemy and knows he must either kill or be killed. So a godly man opposes sin as the deadly enemy of his soul. He knows that he is now grappling for his salvation. I believe there is no man among you who does not now and then oppose sin, but if you do it only jestingly this opposition is worth nothing.

Second, a man may oppose corruptions sparingly. It may be that some of you resist and oppose corruptions. You see sin to be sin and labor to oppose it, but you do it sparingly. You will not sin too much. You deal with sin as David did with Absalom, telling others to deal gently with him. So it may be that you deal gently with your sins and oppose them sparingly. But a mortified man accosts his lusts with a holy cruelty. He will show sin no mercy, nor give any quarter to his lusts. His sins will not spare him; therefore he will not spare them.

Third, you have an unmortified heart if you oppose sin partially, resisting some sins but sparing others, your beloved lusts. It may be that you oppose drunkenness, and yet will permit yourself in other sins such as false weights or measures or being deceitful in your shop or trade. It may be that you oppose adultery and uncleanness, yet yield to and indulge other lusts in your bosom. But mortification is like death upon the body, which seizes all the vitals and parts of the body. So if you do not oppose all sin, you are a stranger to mortification. You are to do with your sins as Saul did with regard to the Amalekites. Though he killed the Amalekites, he saved Agag their king and the best of the sheep and cattle, whereas he should have destroyed them all. Though you oppose some sins, yet if you harbor and indulge others in your hearts, as Saul by his partiality lost his kingdom, so you, by your indulgence and partiality to some profitable or delightful sins, will lose your souls. As Saul's sparing of Agag cost him his kingdom, so the sparing of any one lust in your soul will cause you to lose the kingdom of heaven.

Fourth, a man may oppose sin hypocritically or upon false ends and grounds, when he opposes sin not because it hinders him from doing good, but because it hinders him from receiving good. He never opposes any sin because this or that lust hinders him in prayer and interrupts him in holy duties, such as hearing or reading; because it hinders him from good; or because it keeps him from heaven and happiness and glory, but only because it hinders him receiving from the good he hopes for and expects. He does not oppose sin because it is repugnant to the glory of God, but because it impugns and crosses his expectation. So a man may oppose sin in these four senses and yet be unmortified.

Fifth, a man may oppose sin slavishly. If merely the fear of hell and the wrath to come make you resist a present corruption, you would not care what sins you committed if hell and punishment did not follow them. A man opposes sin slavishly when he does it merely because God punishes sin, not because He hates it; not because sin has a condemning power; not because it carries a defiling power with it; not because sin is against the avenging justice of God; not because it is against the holiness and purity of God; but because there is a hell *for* sin, not because there is a hell *in* sin. A godly man opposes sin filially: if there were no devil in hell and no punishment for sin, yet a godly man would hate it because of the filthiness of it, because there is a hell in sin which he sees to be worse than hell itself.

Sixth, a man may oppose sin constrainedly. Many men oppose corruption in their heart, but it is because they have terrors and grips and gnawing of conscience upon them. They have so much light in their natural conscience that they cannot yield to sin without some reluctance. They would gladly shake off the gnawing of their conscience and lull it to sleep that it might not do its office, so that they might sin securely and peaceably. Such an opposition as this is no argument at all of mortification.

Seventh, a man may oppose corruptions faintly and slowly. It may be that you resisted corruptions resolutely at first, but afterward you grew faint, weary, and remiss in your opposition. Heretofore you could not endure drunkenness or uncleanness, but now you are more pliable and yielding to sin. Many men in opposing sin are like the Frenchmen in battle, of whom it is related that there are no men in the world who will give a fiercer onset and charge; but if they meet with a good repulse from the enemy, then their courage is cooled and daunted and no men are more cowardly and fearful than they. So it may be that some of you are very resolute at first against sin, but if the devil comes upon you with a fierce charge, then you grow faint-hearted and yield and comply with sin. Just so Balaam did in Numbers 22. When Balak sent for Balaam to curse Israel, at first he refused to go (verse 13). He said to the princes of Balak, "Get you into your land, for the Lord refuseth to give me leave to go with you." In verse 18 he said,

"If Balak would give me his house full of silver and gold, I cannot go beyond the word of the Lord my God, to do less or more." Why now, you would think Balaam to be a very good man, but when the king sent for him the third time he was ready to go. But you may say, "God bade him go; therefore he is excusable." Verse 20: "And God came unto Balaam at night, and said unto him, 'If the men come to call thee, rise up and go with them.' " Yet when Balaam went in the morning, God's anger was kindled against him because he went. Now how can this be? Can God be angry with a man for doing that which He bids him do? I answer that God bade him go conditionally: "If the men come to call thee, rise up and go with them," but we do not read that the men called him.

God bade him go, but He did so as you bid an untoward child to do a thing when he insists on having his own will: "Well, do it if you will; take your own course and see what will come of it." So God said to Balaam, "If you need to go, if you love their money and the wages of unrighteousness so well, go with them and see what will come of it."

God bade him go not to curse, but to bless Israel. Now, the text says, God was angry with Balaam because he went. God bade him go to bless Israel, but he went with an intent to curse them; and that was the reason why God was angry with him.

Thus it may be that some of you may with Balaam refuse to satisfy your lusts once or twice, and yet embrace them the third time; though you oppose sin resolutely at first, yet if you yield to cowardice and grow faint afterwards, it is a sign that your heart is not yet mortified.

Eighth, a man may oppose sin politically. A man may be said to oppose sin in two ways: when a man opposes sin more because an *outward* judgment follows that sin than because a *spiritual* judgment does.

In Genesis 20, Abimilech was at risk of abusing Sarah, Abraham's wife; yet when he knew her to be Abraham's wife, he let her go and sent to Abraham and said, "Why is it that you did not tell me she was your wife? You might have caused me to have brought evil upon the kingdom by it." A wicked man may oppose sin because it brings evil upon his body or house or kingdom, but not because sin is a dishonor to God. A man opposes sin politically when it is merely upon a carnal consideration.

A man may oppose one sin so that he may harbor another sin with less suspicion. You may leave your drunkenness so that you may keep other sins without being suspected. Herein you play the politician to damn your own soul.

Thus I am done with these eight particulars wherein you see that you may oppose sin jestingly, sparingly, partially, hypocritically, slavishly, constrainedly, faintly, and politically. If you go no further in opposing your lusts, you cannot claim a work of mortification on your hearts.

This much shall serve to explain the first ground of wicked men's mistaking their opposition to corruptions.

GROUND 2. "Oh, but," says another, "I not only oppose corruptions, but, blessed be God, I restrain and keep them under so that they do not break forth into acts in my life and conversation. Therefore, I hope my heart is mortified and all things well with me, seeing that I have a power enabling me to restrain and keep under my corruptions."

In answer to this, I must acknowledge that this is a good step in the way to heaven for a man both to oppose and restrain his lusts from coming forth into action. Yet I have three words to say to you so that you may not be mistaken.

The first is this: a man may restrain a sin merely from the principles and dictates of nature. The power of nature may restrain a man from the commission of some sins. We read that Socrates professed he was addicted to chastity, that he never had a lustful thought and wanton glance with his eye, nor a lascivious carriage of his body all of his lifetime; yet he was a heathen man. Cato was so afraid of drunkenness that he professed he never drank so much but he could drink more even to refresh nature. Such men as these go beyond many Christians.

Second, lusts may be restrained from the force of religious education. For example, we read in 2 Kings 12:2 of Jehoash. The text says, "He did that which was right in the sight of the Lord, all the days of Jehoiada the priest." All the while Jehoiada lived Jehoash did that which was right in the sight of the Lord, but when Jehoiada died, then Jehoash did wickedly. Sin was restrained in him while he lived under the tuition of a good man, but afterwards it broke out.

Similarly, it may be that you who are under masters and tutors, who have a strict eye over you, all the while you are servants sin may be restrained in you, but when you come to be your own men, to go where you will and do what you will, then it may be that you will run out into many sins which now are restrained by education, not through mortification.

Third, a man may restrain his lusts and abstain from some sins merely because of the terror and trouble of conscience that lies upon him. His conscience tells him that there is a hell prepared for him if he goes on in such a course or commits such and such sins. He has the flashing of hellfire, as it were, in his face, so that he dares not commit such a sin.

Suppose a dog had a bone lying before him and his master's stick over him; if he snatches at the bone, his master knocks him and makes him let it alone. The dog fears his master's staff or else he would have the bone. So it is with a wicked man: were it not for the gnawing and terrors of his conscience that troubles and frightens him, he would make no bones of falling into any sin or wickedness whatsoever. Such a restraint as this does not in any way argue that your sins are mortified.

I shall show you further that there may be a restraint of sin in three particular cases, and yet sin is not mortified, though it is restrained.

CASE 1. Perhaps your restraint from a sin is a burden to you, not voluntary but burdensome and fully sore against your will. It may be that through sickness and weakness of body you cannot commit some sins and this is a grief and burden to you. If it is this way, you have a very unmortified heart.

A godly man is restrained from sin willingly. He counts it his happiness, and a great mercy, to have sin restrained; therefore, examine your own hearts. If it is a grief of heart to you to have your sins restrained, so that you cannot follow your whores or your drunkenness, and the satisfaction of your lusts, to run out into all manner of sins—if it is this way with you, you have no spark of mortifying grace in you.

CASE 2. Sin is not mortified if your restraint from a sin makes you run out with more vehement eagerness after that sin, when the restraint is removed, than ever you did before. It may be that you are restrained by a watchful eye that is over you so that you cannot follow after whoring or drunkenness or Sabbath-breaking, or it may be that you are sick and so not able to do it.

But now, if after these restraints are removed you then run out after these sins, it is a sad sign that your heart is unmortified, and that you are at the next door to damnation and reprobation, for the restraint of a sin has made you more violent and eager after it when the restraint is removed.

CASE 3. Sin is not mortified if the restraint of sin reaches only to outward and grosser acts of sin, but not to inward and secret evils. For, as I told you before, you may abstain from and keep under great sins by the very light and instinct of nature, as did Socrates and Cato, who were heathens. Therefore, unless your restraint of sin extends to inward and bosom sins as well as to open and notorious crimes, you cannot conclude that the power of mortifying grace is upon your heart.

The very light of nature teaches and convinces a man that he should not lie or steal, nor swear, nor be drunk or unclean; yet a wicked man may keep under other great crying sins, for they do not discern these to be sins in themselves. They do not look upon inward evils to be any evil at all. Therefore, we read that Aristotle counted many things to be virtues which the Scripture condemns as vices. Heathens look upon jesting as a virtue, which Paul tells us is a sin. Therefore, he counsels us to avoid foolish talking and jesting as things not convenient.

Aristotle counted it a magnanimity for a man to be highly conceited and opinionated of himself, as deserving great places of honor and repute in the world; but Paul looked upon it as pride of heart for a man to think highly and nobly of himself.

I only hint these things to you so that you may see the light of nature is too dark and dim to discover many sins, especially if they are small and inward evils. You may keep under open and notorious sins, and yet never have the power of grace upon your hearts. Mortification lays a restraint upon inward and secret sins, so that a man's whole endeavors are bent against them as well as against grosser evils.

Thus, I have done with the two first grounds of mistakes in wicked men whereby they think their corruptions are mortified when indeed they are not.

Sermon 6

"But if ye through the Spirit do mortify the deeds of the body, ye shall live." Romans 8:13

The Third Ground of Mistakes of Deluded Men

I now come to the third ground of mistakes that make deluded men think their sins are mortified when they are not. Another man will tell you that he goes further than both the former two: "I not only oppose corruptions and restrain some outward acts of sin, but I am a man who has quite left my sins. I was a man (it is true) given to uncleanness in times past, but I am a chaste man now. I have been a drunkard before, but I am a sober man now. Therefore, I hope my corruptions are mortified in me."

I confess this is a very fair plea that you make. I say to you as Christ said to the lawyer, "Thou art not far from the kingdom of heaven." But let me tell you that if you go no further and do no more, you will never come forth. Therefore I shall show you, so that you may not deceive and delude yourself, that there may be a dereliction and leaving of sins in many particulars in which a man has been formerly addicted, yet that man is a stranger to mortification in three cases: if he leaves sin from a wrong principle; if he leaves sin in a wrong manner; and if he leaves sin from a wrong end.

CASE 1. You are a stranger to mortification if you

leave those sins where you were formerly addicted from a wrong principle, among which there are these four:

First, a man may leave a sin because he is devoid of strength and ability to act out that sin, and this is a wrong principle. Suppose a man has been given in time past to uncleanness and sinful pleasures with women, but now has grown old and sickly and so he leaves it off. This is not mortifying grace; but he leaves this sin because his body is disabled, and the vigor of his spirit is gone so that he cannot commit this sin any longer; therefore, this is no thanks to the man at all.

It may be that another man has been strongly inclined to drunkenness in times past, but now his means are spent, and his money falls short, and he wants wherewithal to follow his old course. Therefore he leaves it off. Be the sin what it will, if you leave it upon such a principle as this you are a stranger to mortification.

Second, you are a stranger to mortification if you leave a sin because you are left devoid of an opportunity to commit that sin, if you have not secrecy, nor security, nor convenience to commit such a sin. You cannot do what you would do. You cannot walk in those ways you have a desire to walk in. This is another wrong principle for forsaking sin.

Third, you are a stranger to mortification if you leave sin because motions and temptations to such a sin leave you. Beloved, the devil does not always suggest the same temptations to a man. It may be that he prompts and solicits you to lust today and to drunkenness tomorrow. The devil does not always harp upon the same stirring in tempting you. Now it may be that you have left some sins, but it is because the devil's temptations to those sins have left you; and this is not praiseworthy, for you may leave sin upon this principle and yet be a stranger to mortification.

Some men have been given to wantonness and uncleanness in their youth, and afterwards, in their middle age, the devil suspending his instigation for a while, they have been wholly averse and opposite to that sin so as not to endure a lascivious look or an unchaste affection. Yet, through renewed temptations from Satan, they have been enticed to run after the same sin with as much greediness and delight as ever. The devil may leave you, and you may leave a sin for a long time, yet afterwards with a fresh temptation fall into the same sin again.

Fourth, a man may leave sin upon this ground: he knows that if he does not the terrors of conscience will not leave him. He knows that if he goes on in a course of swearing, lying, cheating, and defrauding in his shop, sabbath-breaking, writing the sermon he hears on that day in his book and writing them in the devil's book all the week after; if he still follows after the satisfaction of his lusts, he knows that his conscience will accuse him and scare him more and more. Therefore he will restrain and bridle his corruptions awhile until his conscience is bridled and pacified. Therefore it is observable that the Scripture compares an unmortified man to a dog that returns to his vomit.

In 2 Peter 2:20–22, the Apostle speaks of some who had gone so far in Christianity that they had escaped the pollution of the world through the knowledge of the Lord and Savior Jesus Christ, but yet were again entangled therein and overcome. The text says that it is happening to them according to the true proverb: the dog is turned to his own vomit again, and the sow that was washed has returned to wallowing in the mire.

What is the meaning of this? There is much of the mind of God in this passage. A man who has once left his sinful course, and afterwards follows it again, is like a dog that returns to his vomit and a sow to wallowing in the mire.

Now you know that when a dog has a pain or qualm upon his stomach (which he is often subject to), he disgorges himself. So when a wicked man's conscience troubles and accuses him, he leaves and forsakes his sin. But as the dog, when he is rid of his pain, returns and licks up his vomit again, a wicked man, when his conscience is quiet and the horror of it over, returns to his old sins again and commits them with greater delight and complacency than ever.

Thus you see in four particulars that if you leave sin upon any of these wrong grounds and principles, you are a stranger to mortification.

CASE 2. If you leave your corruptions in a wrong manner (which may be done in several ways), you are a stranger to this work of mortification.

First, you leave sin in a wrong manner when you forsake one sin to allow yourself another. I have read of one who was given to drunkenness, yet by reading the lectures of Plato, which condemn and speak against that sin, he was never drunk again. Yet he fell into other sins equally bad. So if you forsake one sin and embrace another, this is no mortification; rather, mortification involves a seizure upon the whole body of sin.

A man in his youth may be given to the sin of wantonness, and when he is old may change that into the sin of worldly-mindedness. Again, some part of a man's life may be given to prodigality, and at another time he may leave that and fall into the sin of niggardliness and parsimony. He may also be guilty of the sin of hypocrisy, while another falls into the sin of apostasy and open profanation.

Naturalists tell us that every year the serpent casts off his skin, but has another in place of it; he still is a serpent. So some of you may cast off your old sins, yet embrace others in place of them. This is only sin exchanged, not mortified. The exchanging of a sin is not the subduing of it. That sin which heretofore you were much addicted to may be now asleep, and another sin alive and just as vigorous and active in your heart. This exchanging of your sins falls short of mortification.

Second, a man may be said to leave sin in a wrong manner when he only abstains from the gross acts of a sin, but does not leave the inward hankering and desires of his soul after that sin. Augustine, for a season, left the sin of incontinence, but he confessed that he had still secret hankering in his soul for that sin.

If you do not extinguish in your souls those longing desires after a sin, you do not leave the sin. For example, a man may leave the outward act of uncleanness, and yet harbor in himself adulterous thoughts, wanton looks, obscene words, and lascivious gestures. His heart may be like the devil's anvil whereon he fashions an abundance of speculative wickedness; therefore this is not mortification, for that makes you leave not only the outward act of sin, but also that secret delight and complacence you took in that sin. This is a second wrong manner of leaving sin.

Third, a man leaves sin in a wrong manner when he only leaves open, outward, and crying sins, yet indulges himself in some inward and secret evils. This is but leaving sin by halves. We read of many heathens who have restrained themselves from falling into gross acts of sin. Socrates was so free from uncleanness that he was never observed to have a wanton glance with his eye or a lascivious gesture with his body, yet he was a heathen still. Cato was so averse to drunkenness that he never drank so much as to satisfy his nature. Though Aristotle knew and abstained from the grosser acts of sin, yet he was a stranger to small and lesser sins, and he could not discover them. That which he counted a virtue, Paul reckoned to be a sin, such as foolish talking and jesting. Paul looked upon them as things not convenient, though Aristotle esteemed them as virtues.

Also, for a man to think highly of himself Aristotle counted as magnanimity, which Paul looked upon as pride; and the reason is that though they knew by the light of nature what was bad in terms of gross sins, yet they did not know, neither were they acquainted with smaller sins so as to discover and avoid them.

Fourth, a man leaves his sins in a wrong manner

when he does it unwillingly, when he leaves his sins as the mariners do their goods when they are in a great storm and the ship is heavy laden with rich commodities. The master tells them that unless they throw over some of their goods, they will lose all and be cast away. Now those who own the goods will be as ready as any to cast them overboard, not because they do not love them, but because they love their lives better. So when wicked men see hellfire and a river of brimstone before them, which they must be cast into unless they leave and forsake their sins, upon these grounds they do it, though it is very unwillingly.

Fifth, a man leaves a sin in a wrong manner when he does it with a reservation and purpose of mind to commit that sin again at another time. It may be that he reasons thus with himself: "I have delighted much in drunkenness and good fellowship, but now I am sick and weak and not able to follow it; but if ever I am well again I will take my old course and go to my good company again."

Another may think thus with himself: "I have now left the sin of uncleanness by reason of my weakness of body and inability to act, but if I recover I will go to that pleasure again." Now when a man leaves his sins in such a manner as this, his sins will break in again upon his soul like an inundation of mighty water, with more power and force than ever they did before.

Sixth, a man leaves his sins in a wrong manner when he leaves them without any sound humiliation and sorrow for the sins he has forsaken. Mr. Bolton made a pertinent observation after he had been with one (as he thought) lying upon his deathbed, a man much given to wine and women, an extreme drunkard and a very lascivious man. As the man lay upon his bed, Mr. Bolton asked him whether he had any hopes of heaven or not. "Why, it is true that I have been a drunkard, but now I am none. I have been an adulterer, but now I have left it." But Mr. Bolton observed that he did not express any grief or sorrow or humiliation for the sins he had been guilty of; therefore he asked him whether, if God should restore him to his health again, he would be the same man he was before. He answered, "No, I would not be so for all the world." But it pleased God within a little while to let this man recover; and not many months after he was well he returned to his old sins again as bad as ever.

Hence we see that a bare forsaking of sin for a time is no true mortification. Such a man is not mortified, though he leaves his sins, if he is not truly humbled and grieved for them. Many of you may have left off swearing and lying, but have your sins left humiliation behind them? Has sin left a scar behind it so that you still mourn and grieve for it? If it is not so with you, you cannot have assurance in your heart that you are a mortified man or woman.

Thus, I am done with the second particular, namely leaving sin from a wrong principle and in a wrong manner.

CASE 3. Leaving sin is not an argument of mortifying grace in your heart if you leave it in a wrong manner. And herein I may be near the bosom of many of you. There are six wrong ends a man may leave his sins for, and yet be a stranger to mortifying grace.

First, a man may leave his sins, but the peace of his conscience may not leave him. He knows that unless he leaves his sins the peace of a good conscience will leave him, whereas were it not for breaking his own peace he would not leave his sins even if he broke God's heart by his sins. When a man leaves his sins merely because the peace of his conscience may not leave him, this is one wrong end.

Second, a man may leave his sins only because temporal punishments may leave him, not because God hates sin but because He punishes it. Here sin is left not because it has a defiling power, but because it has a destroying power with it; because of its penalty, not because of its depravity. Some men forbear outward acts of villainy not because the law is against it, but because it punishes such acts. In the same way, they leave sin not because God hates it, but because He punishes it. This is another wrong end of leaving sin.

Third, a man may leave a sin because it stains his honor and reputation before men, not because it is a dishonor to God; because it brings a spot and blemish upon his own name and credit, not because it is a blemish to the glory of God.

Fourth, a man may leave his sins so that the torments of hell will not follow him. He knows that if he continues in a course of wickedness his sins will at last find him out, and the torments of hell will inevitably seize upon him. A wicked man leaves sin because there is a hell following sin, and not because there is a hell in sin. He leaves sin because it is against the avenging wrath of God, not because it is against the holiness and purity of God; not because God has commanded him to leave it, but because there are curses pronounced in the Word of God against it. This is a very false and slavish end for a man to propound to himself in leaving sin.

Fifth, a man may leave a sin so that he may harbor another with less suspicion. This, as I told you before, is to leave sin politically, to forsake some sins that he may be the less suspected in indulging himself in others.

Sixth, a man may leave and abstain from sin merely because he may be accounted a holy, blameless, and religious man in the world. I have read of one who left an ill curse that he was much addicted to so that a friend of his, by whom he hoped and expected an inheritance would be given to him, might have a good opinion of him. A man may leave gross sins so he may be accounted as a new man and a holy man among his neighbors. It is a very base and vile end to leave an evil so that others may have good thoughts of him.

Thus I have in these last two sermons addressed the mistakes that many men run into concerning this great duty of mortification.

I will now add a word of comfort and be done. It may be that what I have said concerning this particular has troubled many a godly and conscientious heart. Perhaps that person thinks his corruptions are not mortified, but that he has left his sins from some wrong principles or in a wrong manner or for some false ends, when there is no such problem.

Therefore, for your comfort, you who are the sons and daughters of God, lift up your heads with rejoicing and gladness if your hearts can bear you witness that you have left your sins from other grounds, and in another manner, and for other ends than wicked men do. You can say you have left your sins not because you want abilities or opportunities—for you have as many of these as Joseph ever had—but through the power of sanctifying grace in your hearts.

You can say, "I have forsaken my sins not because my conscience snarled upon me like a dog and caused the flashes of hellfire in my face, but because the love of Christ constrained me, because Christ shed His blood and paid a dear price for my sins. I have left my sins in a right manner. I have not left one that I might live and allow myself to commit another, but I would leave all sins if I could. I do not leave sin by force and constraint, but the Lord knows that never a poor slave was more willing to come out of the galleys than I am to come out of my sins. There was never a poor prisoner more willing to come out of prison than I am to leave my sins. There is never a lowly beggar on the streets who is more willing to come out of his rags and be clothed in rich apparel than I am to part with my sins, those menstruous rags, that I may be clothed with the long robes of Christ's righteousness."

Oh, the poor souls whose heart can bear witness that it is so with them should not go home with a sad heart, for they are in a happy condition. If your heart bears witness that you have left sin for a right end, not because there is a curse against your lust but because there is a command against them; that you leave sin not because it is against the avenging justice of God, but against the holiness and purity of God; not because there is a hell for sin, but because there is a hell in sin; because of its depravity and defilement, not because of its penalty and destroying nature—if it is this way with you, you may lift up your head with joy, and go away with a sea of comfort upon your heart, in the assurance that God has brought you into a mortified state.

Thus I have, in these six sermons, shown you many weighty truths concerning this great doctrine of mortification. In the next place, I shall give you some general means and directions how you may attain to this duty of mortification—not in particular how you should mortify every particular sin, for that would be a work too tedious to go through, but only in general how you may mortify any lust.

Then I shall handle some other cases of conscience as to whether a man may fall into a sin after it is mortified or not, and several other cases.

Sermon 7

"But if ye through the Spirit do mortify the deeds of the body, ye shall live." Romans 8:13

Means and Helps to Mortification

I come now to one more query touching this doctrine of mortification. I think I hear a poor perplexed soul (who has heard all the sermons I have preached upon this text) say, "I confess that all you have said and spoken in reference to this duty of mortification is but a looking glass to let me see into my own heart. Whereby I discover that my heart is not yet mortified and that I have a great many lusts and corruptions still unsubdued in me; therefore, I would gladly know how I might be enabled to mortify my sins and to overcome my corruptions."

Therefore, this shall be the next query I shall handle, namely to show you what means and helps you may use in mortifying and keeping under those corruptions that trouble you and prevail over you. In prosecuting this, I shall not only run into particulars on how to mortify every lust, but shall give you some general helps and means to keep under the sin, whatever it will be. I shall name eight in all.

1. Be very careful to shun and avoid all occasions to which you are most strongly addicted. When a man lies under a feverish distemper or ague, though he may eat some slender meats, yet the doctor tells

him he must take heed of strong meats. Now if he does not abstain from them awhile (which will feed and heighten the distemper), he can expect no help or cure. So you must shun all those things that may stir up or give any occasion to your lusts. You must take heed of going near these as well as of stumbling blocks. If you would not fall, you must avoid all occasions of evil, as the Apostle says in Jude 23: "hating even the garment spotted of the flesh."

There is a remarkable passage to this purpose in Numbers 6:3–4, where the Lord makes a law that the Nazarites must drink neither wine nor strong drink. In order to do this, the Lord forbade them to eat so much as the kernel or husk of the grape. They were forbidden not only to drink of the juice, but not to eat of the husk of the grape because that might be an occasion or incitement to taste the wine of the grape. They were to avoid all occasions of committing that sin. So the people of God should not only be on guard against actual sin, but against all occasions or provocations to any sin.

It was Pharaoh's instigation to Moses (when he and the children of Israel were going out of Egypt) that he should leave his children and servants behind him. But he was resolute, and would have them with him. Pharaoh bade him go, but leave his cattle, sheep, and oxen behind. In Exodus 10:26, Moses told him there should not be a hoof left behind. He knew that if they had left anything behind, it might have been an allurement to the children of Israel to hanker after Egypt again. The way to mortify a sin is to avoid all occasions that may induce you to commit that sin to which you are addicted.

2. Another general means to mortify sin is this: withstand a lust or corruption in its very first risings and workings in your heart. If you give way to a sin, the more power it will have over you and the more difficult it will be to subdue it; therefore, crush the cockatrice in the egg. It is an easier matter to keep an enemy out than to thrust him out when he is already in. You should keep your souls, as it were, in a garrison. Do not give way to sin, but resist and oppose it in its first motion.

3. Another means is this: bend the greatest strength of your heart in importunate prayer to God against the corruption that troubles you the most. Paul, in 2 Corinthians 12:8, had a thorn in his flesh, a messenger of Satan to buffet him; and he sought the Lord thrice that it might depart from him. In Psalm 56:9 David says, "When I cry unto Thee, then shall mine enemies turn back." So when we call out to God, it is the way to make our lusts turn from us. There is never a mortified man who has not been a praying man. Subduing lust can never be obtained without prayer, for prayer is the sword of the Spirit whereby we can conquer and overcome our corruptions. When you grow most remiss and careless and formal in prayer, then you are most of all troubled with unmortified lusts and corruptions. Isaiah 64:6–7 the church complains, "We all fade as a leaf; our iniquities, like the wind, have taken us away, and there is none that calleth upon Thy name." We are carried headlong by our lusts as the dust is hurled by the wind. The reason is that there is none who calls upon His name.

A contemporary author has given us this rule: either your sins will make you leave praying or your praying will make you leave sinning. If you continue still to pray against sin, in time prayer will mortify and kill your lusts and corruptions. This is the third means.

4. If you would keep under your corruptions, then keep in your memory some special sentences of Scripture which most express and vehemently forbid those sins to which you are most strongly inclined. This is an excellent way to fence your heart against any corruptions. David said in Psalm 119:11, "I have hid Thy word in my heart, that I might not sin against Thee," that is, "I have hidden Thy special word in my heart against my beloved and darling sin, so that when I am tempted to commit it I might consider your express command against that sin."

Thus when our Savior was tempted by the devil, He told him, "It is written that you shall not tempt the Lord thy God." He convinced him from Scripture of his sin.

If you had in your thought some express places of Scripture against those sins you are most inclined to, this would help you in subduing your sins. Therefore, look over the whole Bible and choose those places of Scripture that most dreadfully threaten that sin. For example, if you are given to uncleanness consider this: "He that goes in to a harlot, he shall not take hold of the paths of life," and "whoremongers and adulterers God will judge" (Hebrews 13:4). So for any other sin you are addicted to, recollect and gather together the most direct Scriptures that speak against it and condemn it.

5. Exercise yourself and join yourself to solemn

fasting for that particular sin you are most inclined to. In 1 Corinthians 9:25–27 the Apostle says, "He that striveth for the mastery is temperate in all things; so fight I, not as one that beateth the air, but to keep under my body and bring it into subjection." The way to tame an unruly heart is by fasting and prayer; a conscientious use of these duties will be a great means to give corruptions its fatal blow. Fasting and prayer are the slaughter-houses of sin.

I may say of sin as Christ said of the devil in Matthew 17:21: all kinds of devils are not alike, and "this kind will not go out but by fasting and prayer." Some sins will not go out of us by ordinary means, but by fasting and prayer.

6. If all these means will not prevail for the subduing of your lusts, then use this help: lay yourself under a solemn covenant unto God that you will, through the strength of Christ, forbear those sins that reign and rule in you. I say, resolve in the strength of Christ; for all your covenants and promises must be made in the strength of God's covenant and promise. There is no man who makes a vow or promise to God in the strength of Christ to subdue his lusts but he will do it sooner or later. If you have used all other means to bridle your lusts, and they prove ineffectual, in this case we should bind ourselves to God in an oath that in the strength of Christ we will forsake our sins.

OBJECTION. But some may say, "If we break this vow, as we are in no way able to perform it, this will be a double sin." If you are weak and unable to perform this duty, you are insufficient to do any other duty that is required of you.

ANSWER. If you are weak and unable to perform this duty, you are as insufficient to do any other duty that is required of you. But if God helps you to carry on in this work by His strength, then you may perform it; and a vow is God's ordinance. If you make a vow in Christ's strength, He will assist you in it to accomplish it.

7. When you go about this work of mortification, do not bend your strength against one particular act of sin, but set your whole strength against the whole body of sin.

The way to keep a tree from growing is not to cut off the branches, but to pluck it up by the roots. If you would mortify a lust, you must strike at the whole body of sin and labor to bewail and subdue it. Therefore when David, in Psalm 51, came to humble his soul before God for the sin of adultery, he did not say, "Lord, forgive me this sin only," but in the beginning of the Psalm he lamented the whole body of sin that was in him. "Oh, Lord," said he, "I was shapen in iniquity, and in sin did my mother conceive me" (verse 5).

8. Would you mortify and keep under sin in your heart? Then meditate much upon Christ's death and your own. These are effectual means to kill and keep under sin.

Meditate upon Christ's death. Think to yourself: "Shall I live in those sins that the Lord Jesus Christ died to redeem me from? Shall I harbor those lusts in my heart that shed the blood of my dear Savior? Shall I not kill those sins that killed Christ, and see the blood of those lusts that spilled the blood of the Lord Jesus Christ?" Such considerations will make a man refrain from sin and subdue it. Meditating on the death of Christ is an effectual means to put us to crucifying and killing our lusts.

Not only the thought of Christ's death, but the thought of your own death, too, will stir you up to mortification. Consider with yourself, "I must not live always here. I must die sooner or later, and after death comes judgment, when I must give an account for everything done in the body, whether it is good or evil; and those sins that are now sweet and delightful to me will, when I come to die, be as gall and wormwood to me then, and as gravel in my belly." This result would certainly be bitterness in the latter end, and, if we seriously considered this truth, it would be a great means to keep under sin.

USE OF CONSOLATION. I have briefly run over these eight particular directions on how to mortify sin. It remains now to wind up what has been said with a comforting use, a use of consolation. It may be that there are many conscientious souls who hear me this day whose consciences bear them witness that they have not been enemies to their own souls in this particular, but have labored to oppose and mortify their lusts. Yet they find the workings of corruption to be very strong in their hearts. To you, I have these five words to say:

1. Take this for your comfort: though you use the utmost endeavors to mortify sin, yet you cannot withstand the existence of sin in you, but only hinder its reigning in your heart. Sin will be in your soul, as I told you, like those beasts spoken of in Daniel 7:12 whose dominion was taken away, but

their lives were prolonged for a little season. The existence of sin will not be taken away, though its reigning power is taken away. In 2 Corinthians 4:7, the Apostle compares our bodies to earthen vessels, and the filth of sin that is in us can never be fully cleansed and washed away until these vessels are broken in pieces and our bodies are laid in the dust. Until we shake off these bodies of flesh, we shall never shake off our bodies of sin. Therefore, this may be a great comfort to you: God does not expect you to root out all presence of sin, but only to keep down the reigning of sin in you.

2. Take this for your comfort: if you use all conscionable means to bridle your lusts, you may be confident that sooner or later grace shall get the victory over sin. Sin may be a combatant, but it shall never be a conqueror. Grace in Scripture is compared to oil, and corruptions are compared to water. As oil will swim to the top—you cannot keep it under the water—so grace will in time get the victory over your corruptions. Christ will not break the bruised reed, nor quench the smoking flax, until He has brought forth judgment into victory (Isaiah 42:3). By a bruised reed and smoking flax are meant weak Christians; and Christ will not discourage such though their graces do not burn into a flame. If they but smoke He will not quench them until they have brought forth judgment into victory, that is, until those sparks and small beginnings of grace in them burn into a flame and become victorious over their corruptions. A reed is weak by itself, but a bruised reed is weaker. Yet this shall not be broken until the work of grace is perfected in your soul and becomes

victorious over all the opposition and temptations of Satan.

3. Remember this for your comfort: if you conscientiously make use of those means that the Lord has sanctified for the mortifying of your sins, then, even if, notwithstanding all, your sins prevail over and overcome you, in this case the Lord will hold you guiltless. I might urge that place to you which I quoted the last Lord's day concerning the law of God touching a damsel in Deuteronomy 22:25–27, which was that the adulterer should be put to death. But, God says, if the damsel was walking in the field and a man came to her and defiled her, if she strove against him and cried out, then the damsel shall be guiltless, but the man shall die the death.

When the devil spiritually rapes you, if your soul can bear you witness that you cried out to God for help, and struggled and strove against the corruption with all your might and strength to suppress and keep them under, and yet you could not prevail but the devil overmatched you, in this case know that God will count you guiltless.

4. Take this for your comfort: God will never damn you for that sin which in the whole course of your life you used all possible means to subdue and destroy. You may plead with God when you come to die, "Oh, Lord, will you condemn and throw me into hell for that sin which I have labored all my lifetime to throw out of my heart?" I might, in this case of resisting corruptions, make use of what naturalists tell us concerning the crocodile, which is a serpent that, if it sees a man afraid of him and running from him, then takes courage and runs after the man and

kills him. But if a man opposes and fights with the crocodile, it will then grow faint-hearted and run away and the man kills him. So here, if you are faint-hearted and yield to every temptation, and will not grapple with those incursions that sin makes upon you, then sin will overcome you and kill you. But if you oppose and pursue sin, and bend all your strength against it so that if you had more tears to shed or more prayers to make or more strength to put forth, you would employ them all against sin; if it is so, my soul for yours, O man, your corruptions shall never be your ruin. Though the devil forces sin upon you, if you use all possible means to resist it the Lord will hold you guiltless.

5. Take this for your comfort: the disturbing and troubling of your heart by a sin argues that sin to be mortified more than unmortified, provided that as your sin stirs in your heart, so your resolutions and supplications against those sins stir in your heart, too. If sin fights against you, you must strive against it in your resolutions and protestations against it. Though it may keep a great deal of stir in your heart, yet it may rather argue that sin is dying rather than living and reigning in you and prevailing over you.

Thus I am done with the dispatch of the first doctrine, namely, that the mortification of corruption is a necessary qualification required in all who would attain salvation.

Sermon 8

"But if ye through the Spirit do mortify the deeds of the body, ye shall live." Romans 8:13

Mortification Is a Work of the Spirit

I come now to make further entrance into the second doctrine presented in the second sermon. "If you through the spirit do mortify the deeds of the body, you shall live." From these words I noted to you that the mortification of corruption is wrought in us by the strength of Christ's Spirit, not our own.

Before I come to handle the cases of conscience necessary to the prosecution of this point, I shall first prove to you by two demonstrations that mortification of corruption is wrought in us by the Spirit of God.

DEMONSTRATION 1. Because the sanctification of a man's nature is the proper and peculiar work or office of God's Spirit, hence the Spirit of God is called the Holy Ghost since its proper office is to make a man holy.

Now, mortification is but one part of sanctification, for sanctification consists of two parts: mortification, or a dying unto sin, and vivification, or a living unto God. Therefore, if sanctification in general is the work of God's Spirit, then mortification must be the work of the Spirit also.

And hence it is that you often find this phrase

added to the Spirit of God: "the sanctification of the Spirit." 1 Peter 1:2: "Elect according to the foreknowledge of God the Father, through sanctification of the Spirit." So in 1 Corinthians 6:11: "And such were some of you, but ye are washed, but ye are sanctified, but ye are justified in the name of the Lord Jesus and by the Spirit of our God."

If mortification is a part of sanctification and the Spirit of God carries on the whole work of sanctification, it must carry on this part of it, mortification.

DEMONSTRATION 2. This appears to be so because it is only the Spirit of God who can savingly enlighten a man's mind, convince his judgment, and make him see the evil of sin. A man will never kill sin until he is persuaded of the evil and danger of it. Therefore, you read in John 16:8: "For this cause God hath sent His Spirit into the world, that He might convince the world of sin." A man will never seek after a cure until he is sensible of his disease. So you will never go about the extirpation of sin until you are sensible of the danger and guilt of your sins. You will never be convinced of the danger and evil of sin unless the Spirit of God enlightens you. The work of mortification is wholly ascribed to the Spirit of God because only He can convince us of the evil of sin so as to make us hate and abhor it and strive against it.

I shall now fall upon the discussion of four needful cases of conscience touching this point. The text says, "If you through the Spirit." The words imply that there is another kind of mortification that is not wrought by the help of the Spirit, but by the power of a man's own good nature or education.

Therefore I shall show you the difference between corruptions mortified by the power of the Spirit of God and corruptions merely restrained by the power of nature.

Next, I shall show you how you may be satisfied in your own consciences that you have mortified your corruptions.

Then I shall show you whether falling often into the same sin may be consistent with mortification.

And finally I shall discuss the symptoms that show what is a man's bosom and darling sin.

CASE 1. Wherein lies the difference between a corruption merely restrained by the power of nature and a lust truly mortified by the Spirit of God?

ANSWER. I shall lay down eight apparent differences.

First, a corruption merely restrained by the power of nature only makes a man forbear the act of sin for the present but does not put into the heart a hateful disposition against that sin. It is the same as with a thief in prison: he may be restrained from a sin because he cannot act it out, but yet he loves the sin (it may be) as well as he ever did. So a man may for a time refrain from the act of sin and yet have no inward hatred implanted in his heart against that sin.

Balaam gave two peremptory answers to Balak's messengers that he would not go down to curse Israel; and yet at last he went because he loved the "wages of unrighteousness" (2 Peter 2:15).

Where there is a real mortification wrought by the power of the Spirit of God, it is so powerful in your heart that it implants a contrary and hateful disposition to that sin which does not permit it to be committed. You not only leave sin, but abhor it. There is not only a cessation from sin, but an indignation against it; therefore, judge yourselves by this difference.

Second, the restraint of sin by the power of nature reaches only to more gross and palpable sins, but not to inward and bosom lusts. By the power of nature, a man's conscience may give him strength and control over gross and visible acts of sin, but it does not extend as far as to secret and bosom sins.

Mortifying grace wrought in us by the Spirit of God reacts so far as to seize upon inward sins as well as outward ones. In Colossians 3:5 the Apostle says, "Mortify, therefore, your members which are upon the earth: fornication, uncleanness," and so on; not only fornication in the act, but uncleanness in the thought, concupiscence and inordinate affections. Mortification by the Spirit reaches to crucifying the inward sins; therefore, examine yourselves in this.

It is said in 2 Samuel 24:10 that David's heart smote him after he had numbered the people. Divines can hardly tell what David's sin was in numbering them, unless it was pride or carnal confidence; yet his heart smote him for it. Tender consciences have their hearts smitten for little sins. His heart smote him likewise for cutting off the lap of Saul's garment in 1 Samuel 24:4–5, which was no sin at all, yet he was troubled for it. But a wicked man is never troubled for small sins. Those sins that almost break a godly man's heart never break a wicked man's sleep. Small sins that are as gravel in a godly man's bowels are but as gravel in a wicked man's gloves that never troubles him.

Third, corruption restrained by the power of nature is a violent and compulsive action. A man undergoes it unwillingly and involuntarily. God said to Abimelech in Genesis 20:6, "Abimelech, I also withheld thee from sinning against Me," which implied that there was a strong inclination in him to commit that sin, but God withheld him from doing it. Though a natural heart does not commit a sin, yet it is kept from it unwillingly. Now when a sin is mortified through the strength of the Spirit, then a man willingly surrenders his lusts.

A wicked man may leave sin, but it is as a friend leaves his friend—with a great deal of unwillingness, and he may shed tears at their parting. But a godly man leaves his sins as a poor prisoner leaves his stinking dungeon or a poor beggar his filthy rags, or as a galley slave is glad to leave plying the oar in a galley. God's people shall be a people of willingness in the day of His power, and shall say unto their idols in their indignation, "Get you hence."

Fourth, when a man is restrained from a sin only by the power of nature, when that restraint is taken off he runs after that sin with greater eagerness and greediness than ever he did. In Hosea 7:6 wicked men are compared to an oven. Now you know that fire in an oven, confined within so small a compass, burns very violently. The more a wicked man is restrained from a sin, the more he burns with heat and rage after his lusts. A river that is dammed up runs out with great strength and a mighty torrent when the bank is broken down. Thus it was with Jehoash in 2 Chronicles 24: all the while that Jehoiada the priest lived, Jehoash fell into no great sin, but after the priest died Jehoash's lust broke out and ran down like a mighty torrent into all manner of sin and wickedness. Though Balaam's sin was restrained for a season, afterward he was more greedy to commit it than ever.

When a man has mortifying grace wrought in him by the Spirit of God, his sins are continually dying and decaying, though they are not quite dead. Sin shall never carry that strength and grievousness with it as it has done, and never makes that seizure upon his heart as formerly.

Fifth, a man who is restrained from sin only by the power of nature is merely restrained by carnal considerations. A man may forbear a sin because of the presence of men and not because of the omnipresence of God. When Joseph was tempted to sin, he went higher and said, "How shall I do this great wickedness and so sin against God?"

A man may be restrained from a sin upon this carnal consideration: lest that sin should bring on him temporal judgments. Thus Abimelech did forbear sin in Genesis 20:9. When he knew that Sarah was Abraham's wife, he said to Abraham, "Why didst thou not tell me that she was thy wife? I might have sinned and so have brought sin upon the kingdom." This was what restrained him from sin, not because God would have been offended by it.

But he who mortifies a sin by the Spirit of God abstains from sin upon spiritual considerations such as this: "If I commit this sin, I shall thereby dishonor God and scandalize the gospel and my profession and encourage other sins to break out afresh in me."

Sixth, a man who restrains his sins by the power of nature does it more because of the eternal punishment that is annexed to his sin than because of that internal punishment that is in sin. He abstains from sin not because God is a holy God, but because he is a just God; not because God hates sin, but because He punishes sin; not because there is a hell *in* sin, but because there is a hell *for* and *after* sin.

A truly mortified man forbears sin more for the internal evil there is in sin than for the external punishment that accompanies sin. One said that if hell stood on one side of him and sin on the other, upon a deliberate debate with his own soul he would rather leap into hell than into sin.

Seventh, when a man's corruptions are merely restrained by the power of nature, though they may be restrained for a time, yet if any temptation, allurement, occasion or opportunity is offered him to commit that sin, he will easily close with it and embrace it. In Proverbs 7:22 you read of a young man who passed through the streets in the evening, and there met a woman in the attire of a harlot who tempted him; and it is said that he went after her straightway without any rational debate; never considering whether God saw him or whether God would condemn him for that sin or not, he straightway followed her.

But now a man who has mortified his corruptions by the power of God's Spirit is still opposing sin, and never commits it but against his will. Sin may sometimes overtake him, but he runs from it as fast as he can.

Eighth, when a man has sin restrained by the power of nature, this restriction is irksome and burdensome to him; but the letting out of his heart after the commission of a sin is joyous and gladsome to him. The restraining of a lust is very tedious and troublesome. Proverbs 13:19: "It is an abomination for a fool to depart from evil." On the other hand, it is a matter of joy and gladness to him to be let loose to sin so that he may take his fill with his sinful pleasures. Jeremiah 11:15: "When thou doest evil thou rejoiceth." Habakkuk 3:14: "Their rejoicing is to devour the poor."

But on the contrary, a godly man rejoices and blesses God that he is restrained from committing a sin. In 1 Samuel 25:32, when Abigail came to David and kept him from spilling innocent blood, David blessed the Lord who had sent her to meet him, and blessed Abigail for her advice which kept him from shedding blood. As the restraint of a sin is gladness to a godly man, so falling into a sin is a matter of trouble, sorrow, and tears to him.

It is the same as with those fishes that breed orient pearls: those pearls that grow in the fish are the torment and disease of the fish, but when the pearls are put upon a man they are an ornament and grace to him. So those sins that are matters of joy and delight to the wicked are the burden, sorrow, and trouble of the godly. Therefore, search into your own bosoms and see whether you can distinguish yourselves from those men who have their corruptions restrained in them by the power of nature and not mortified by the Spirit of God.

I am done with this first case of conscience, showing you the difference in these eight particulars between a man whose sins are restrained in him only by the power of nature and a man who has sin truly mortified in him by the Spirit of God. I come now to a second case of conscience, which I hope to dispatch at this time.

CASE 2. "Oh, but," a poor soul may say, "how shall I be satisfied in my own conscience that my sins are truly mortified and my corruptions subdued through the strength of the Spirit?"

ANSWER. I shall give you two clear and infallible evidences of a mortified man.

1. If it be that, with regard to those corruptions that heretofore have been very stirring in you and prevalent over you, when occasions and opportunities of committing those sins are now openly offered you and yet you in no way close with them, this is a certain evidence that those sins are mortified. Formerly, your nature was as tinder to a spark: as soon as it touched it would take. If now, though you have opportunity, secrecy, security, and all the advantages that may be available for committing a sin, yet you abstain from it, this is an unquestionable evidence that sin is mortified.

This was what declared Joseph's sin to be mortified in that when he had opportunity, importunity, secrecy, and advantages, the doors were shut. There was no one else in the house but he and his mistress, and he had hopes of advancement and preferment, too. She would have made him a great man in her house, yet all these allurements could not persuade him to embrace the sin and offend God.

I hope there are many among you who hear me this day who, although you should meet with as many temptations to this sin as Joseph did, and though no eye should see you, yet would not for all the world commit this sin. This argues a work of God's Spirit in your inward man, without which you could never go so far.

2. Another evidence is this: when you make conscience of and are troubled as well for inward and secret sins as for open and gross transgressions; when there is in your heart a resistance against, and true sorrow for, small and secret sins as well as for open and scandalous offenses; when those sins that are no bigger than molehills lie as heavy upon your heart as if they were mountains; and when your conscience can bear you witness that there is no secret lust that makes an incursion upon your soul but that you strive against it and labor to oppose it—this is an undoubted evidence that God has wrought a work of mortification in you by His Spirit.

Sermon 9

"But if ye through the Spirit do mortify the deeds of the body, ye shall live." Romans 8:13

Two More Cases of Conscience

There are yet two more cases of conscience which I intend, God willing, to speak to.

CASE 3. May a man whose lusts and corruptions are truly mortified by the Spirit of God commit and fall often into those sins that have been mortified?

CASE 4. What symptoms may be given of a bosom and beloved sin that is most unmortified in a man?

I shall begin with the first and lay down six particulars by way of answer.

CASE 3. May a man whose lusts and corruptions are truly mortified by the Spirit of God commit and fall often into those sins that have been mortified?

ANSWER 1. We have examples in Scripture of some men who have not fallen again into those sins that are mortified in them. First, in Genesis 38:26 it is said of Judah, after he was convinced of his sin in abusing Tamar, his daughter-in-law, that he acknowledged his offense and he knew her no more. After he saw his sin, he confessed it and fell no more into that sin.

Another good example is Jehoshaphat in 2 Chronicles 20:37. When the prophet Eliezer came to him and told him of his sin of joining himself with Ahaziah, and that the Lord was angry with him for it, after he was reproved he would not bring the guilt of that sin upon him any more. You see in 1 Kings 22:49 that, when Ahaziah said to Jehoshaphat that his servants might go along with Jehoshaphat's servants in the ships, Jehoshaphat would not agree.

ANSWER 2. Take this by way of answer, that we have no express example in all the Bible that a mortified man fell again into that sin which he had been humbled for, and which was subdued and mortified.

It is not my observation only, but the observation of judicious [William] Perkins that in all the examples of the Old and New Testament he does not take notice of one instance where a man who had mortified a sin fell into it a second time. Therefore, if your sins are mortified, and you fall often into the same sins, you are a man without a pattern.

ANSWER 3. Know this further by way of answer. Though there is no example in all the Scripture of a man who fell again into the same gross sin which before he had mortified, yet there are divers examples of good men who have fallen often into the same sin before they knew it to be a sin, before they were sensible of their sin and truly humbled and grieved for it, and seriously considered between God and their own souls what evil they had done. Thus Solomon fell twice and died wickedly before the Lord. Peter fell thrice, one after another, into the sin of denying his Lord and Master. The children of

Israel fell ten times into the sin of murmuring against the Lord according to Numbers 14:22. Before a man has been mortified and truly humbled for a sin, he may fall often into the same sin.

ANSWER 4. Though there is no example for this in all the Scripture, yet according to reason and experience this may be true. A man who has mortified a sin may fall into the same sin that he has repented of and been humbled for. This answer is given by learned Mr. Perkins: "There is nothing in reason and experience that can assure you that a corruption mortified, especially if it is an inward and secret sin, may not break forth again after you have repented of it."

Suppose the sin is passion: though you strive against it and pray to God every day to enable you by His Spirit to subdue and keep it under, yet, notwithstanding this, on some special occasion or when provocation is offered, your passion may break out again. So inward and bosom lusts may break out again after repentance for them.

ANSWER 5. Though there is no example in all the Scripture that a mortified man has fallen into the same sin again after it was mortified, there is nothing in the whole Bible against it that says expressly or by consequence that you cannot fall into the same sins after they are mortified. Therefore, this is something for your comfort.

ANSWER 6. Take this by way of answer: falling into a corruption a second time, the committing of the same sin after it is mortified, argues a great deal of the strength of sin in the soul. Though it does not argue that there is no grace in that soul, it argues that sin and corruptions are very strong there. Here I shall only add a word or two by way of caution and then proceed to the other cases of conscience.

Consider, first, that falling often into the same sin greatly exposes you to obduracy and hardness of heart. Therefore, I dare aver that if you fall often, again and again into the same sin, you lie under a state of hardness of heart; you have no tender and sensible hearts in you.

Consider that falling often into the same sin will cost you many tears and prayers before you obtain peace of conscience. You may obtain pardon, and yet want peace of conscience and assurance of your pardon for a great while.

It is a deadly and dangerous symptom for a man to fall often into the same sins. I do not say it is damnable, but it is a dangerous and deadly symptom, a sign of death upon you. It is in this case as it is with a relapse into the same disease compared to when a man is first sick. The disease feeds upon his ill humor, and if he recovers he is better and healthier afterward. But if the man falls again into the same disease, then the distemper feeds upon the vital spirits whereas before it fed upon the corruption and ill humor in his body. So it is no less dangerous to relapse into the same sins often in regard to your spiritual health.

CASE 4. I now proceed to the next case of conscience: What symptoms may be given of a man's bosom and darling sin, and which of all others is the most predominant and unmortified in his soul?

This is a needful question, and I shall give you ten symptoms by way of discovery whereby you may know which is your beloved or master sin.

1. That sin is your bosom or master sin which you most frequently commit or fall into in the course of your life. As those actions you are most conversant with seize most upon the heart, so that sin you most frequently commit is the most unmortified and beloved sin. Therefore, consider what sin it is that you often fall into, whether uncleanness or drunkenness or deception in your trade, spiritual pride, and so on. That sin you most frequently fall into is your darling and unmortified sin.

2. That sin which you most easily consent and yield to upon every temptation is your bosom sin. Those sins which you oppose and are seldom persuaded to are not your bosom sins, but that which easily besets you, as the Apostle says, is your master sin. Are you easily drawn to drunkenness? Then that is your master sin. Or if to uncleanness, then that is your master sin, and the like. Therefore, I beseech you, beloved, take a survey of your own heart so that you may find what sin is most unmortified in you, and then bend the greatest of your strength against that sin. Look about you and see what sin it is that most easily besets you and is like fire to your nature—that is your master sin.

3. That sin is most unmortified in you that you are most unwilling of all others to part with. Therefore, a bosom sin in Scripture is compared to the right eye and the right hand, which implies that a man's master and beloved sins are as dear to him

as the members of his body. When you are unwilling to leave a sin, conclude that sin to be your master sin.

4. That sin is most unmortified in you which of all other sins most vexes and galls your conscience; for the conscience is God's messenger in you to check you when you are ill and speak peace to you when you do well. If you go on in ways of sin and follow a sinful course, your conscience will haunt you and dog you and never let you be quiet. Now take a view of your own hearts. I dare say there is not a man or woman among you but now and then your consciences check you and convince you that this is an evil course that you follow or the like. Now observe what sin it is that your conscience most checks you for, and that is your bosom and master sin.

5. That sin which of all others most insinuates itself into your heart when you are in the service of God and performing holy duties, that sin which can be so impudent as to intrude upon your heart when you are in the presence of God—that is your unmortified sin. Therefore, beloved, examine your own heart; what sin is it that of all others most haunts you on the Sabbath, and most troubles you when you are performing your duty to God? What sin is it that especially dogs you at church and during sermons and on fasting days? That sin is your master sin.

6. That sin which your enemies most upbraid you for, and your friends most persuade you against, yet you have no power to leave—that is your bosom and beloved sin. As one says well, "I am more beholden to my enemies than to my friends, for when they are

angry with me they tell me of all my faults, and twit me in the teeth with every known sin I am guilty of."

What sin is it that wicked men most upbraid you for and cast in your teeth and your friends most persuade you from, saying, "Oh, friend, walk no more in this path; be not guilty of this sin any more"? That sin which your friends most persuade you from is your master and most unmortified sin. Therefore, I beseech you, beloved, deal impartially with your own soul. In this regard, there are a great many men and women here before the Lord this day. Now let me ask you this question: Do your enemies sometimes upbraid you with such and such a sin, and do your friends persuade you from it, saying, "For the Lord's sake, follow this sinful course no longer, or the like"? You may be confident that this is the sin most unmortified in your heart.

7. The sin that comes most fresh in your mind to trouble and perplex your conscience when you are in the extremity of any affliction, upon your sickbed or deathbed, or when you are in prison or poverty or the like—that sin which most of all troubles your conscience most commonly is your master sin.

You know the story of the sons of Jacob in Genesis 42:21. They were never troubled for their sin against Joseph, their brother, until there was a famine in their own land. They went down into Egypt to buy bread, and there Joseph, their brother, knew them well enough, yet would not disclose himself to them but told them they were spies and were come to see the nakedness of the land, and he cast them into prison. When they were in prison they said to one another, "We are verily guilty concerning our brother, in that we saw the anguish of his soul when he besought us and we would not hear him; therefore, this distress has come upon us." They never thought of this sin for twenty years until they were cast into prison and affliction; then they remembered it and were troubled by it. That sin which most of all galls your conscience in affliction is your master lust.

8. That sin for which of all others you can least bear a reproof is your master sin. It may be that you bear a reproof for some sins, but when a man hits the nail upon the head and reproves you for your master sin you cannot endure that. Hence it is that some divines observe concerning John the Baptist that had he reproved Herod for any other sin but for that of Herodias, his brother Philip's wife (that it was not lawful for him to have her), probably Herod would have let him alone. So if ministers reprove sin only in general, men can bear this well enough; but when they come and tell this man, "You are a drunkard," and another, "You are a whoremonger," or a deceiver or the like, they cannot endure this reproof, which shows that these are their master sins.

In Matthew 21:41, where Christ asked what shall be done to those wicked husbandmen who had killed their master's servants and slain his son, the chief priests and Pharisees answered that he would miserably destroy those wicked men and let out the vineyard to other husbandmen. But when they perceived that Christ spoke this of them, that they should be destroyed, then they cried out, "God forbid" (Luke 20:16). When He only told them in general that these wicked men were worthy to be destroyed, they acknowledged it to be just and right that they should be destroyed, but when they knew He spoke this of them, they could not endure it; and henceforth they labored to kill Jesus.

9. That is your bosom sin that a man most indulges in and knowingly allows himself. Thus Naaman indulged himself in that sin in 2 Kings 5:18; his bowing in the house of Rimmon declared that to be his master sin. That sin which you most indulge in and allow yourself, using the least means against, is your master sin.

10. That sin is your bosom sin to which all other sins give supplies and yield contribution. Suppose pride is your master sin; then you will use deceit in your trade, false lights and false weights, and so forth, all in your business success to uphold your pride. And so with any other master sin.

Thus I am done with the fourth case of conscience. I have only a short use, which shall be by way of caution from the preceding discussion of bosom lusts.

First, I beseech you all, in the fear of God, to take a survey of your own heart to discover which is your master sin. When you have found it out, though you should be watchful against all other sins, especially bend your strength and care against this sin. Be very vigilant and circumspect over your own hearts that you do not fall into this sin. Thus David said, "I have kept myself from mine iniquity" (Psalm 18:23).

Beloved, in that part of your soul against which sin and the devil make the strongest assaults, be sure to put forth the greatest part of your strength against them. Fight not so much against small or great as against your master sin.

Know and consider that it is the greatest hypocrisy in the world to go about to mortify other sins and yet leave your bosom, beloved sin unsubdued. Would not that man abominably dissemble who went about to stop a little leak in a ship and left a great gap unstopped? No less hypocrisy is it for you to strive against small sins and let your great and master sins alone.

Take heed of being mistaken about your bosom lust in conceiving it is mortified when it is not. It may be that wantonness was your bosom sin in your youth, and now covetousness or worldly-mindedness is in your old age. Your bosom sin in your youth may be another in your old age. Take heed of thinking your bosom or master sin is mortified when it is only changed.

When you have found out your bosom lust, then labor to root it out of your heart and subdue it. When your bosom lust burns in your breast like fire, you should especially labor to quench it, strive against it, and mortify it.

Sermon 10

"But if ye through the Spirit do mortify the deeds of the body, ye shall live." Romans 8:13

Special Helps for Special Corruptions

I come now to give you some special helps against some special corruptions. In the last sermon I gave you some helps in general regarding how to mortify sin, but now I shall give you some particular helps against three particular corruptions, namely, how to mortify uncleanness, spiritual pride, and reigning anger (or passion). I cannot think of any other corruptions that make more frequent incursions into the minds of men than these three. One of these I desire to speak to particularly, and I shall speak very briefly to them all.

I shall begin with the first, the sin of uncleanness, and will lay down to you six helps on how to mortify and keep under unclean lusts.

HELP 1. A special help to mortify unclean lusts is to live in a continual and serious mindfulness of the all-seeing eye of God upon you. Indeed, this is a universal remedy against all sin, but the Scripture applies this help specifically to this sin. Therefore, I make use of Job 31:1 where Job says, "I have made a covenant with my eyes; why then should I think upon a maid"? Verse 4: "Does not the Lord see my ways and count all my steps?" Nothing will control our lusts more than the consideration of God's omniscience, that He sees and takes notice of all our ways.

I have heard a story of a maid who was earnestly solicited by a young man to uncleanness. She told him that if he could bring her to a place where no eye might see them, she would yield to his desires. So the young man led her out of one room into another, and at last when he thought they were most secret and retired, he would have had his desire of her. "But," she said, "the eye of God is upon us still. He sees us and takes notice of us." And upon this very consideration they continued chaste all their lives afterward.

HELP 2. Lay a special fence and safeguard upon your outward senses. The Apostle spoke of some in 2 Peter 2:14, who had "eyes full of adultery" and could not cease from sin. Therefore you should set a watch over your eyes. Take heed of wanton and lascivious looks; they are a window that lets a world of lust into the heart. The Lord made a law in Leviticus 14:9 that the leper who was to be cleansed should shave off the hair of his head and his eyebrows. Similarly, there is no way to effectually root out and cleanse yourselves from fleshly lusts as to set a watch over your eyes that they may not look upon vanity. Job said, "I have made a covenant with my eyes." You should keep your eyes from wanton glances if you would control fleshly lusts. Hence we read that Abimelech, in Genesis 20:16, when he surrendered up Sarah, Abraham's wife, to him, said to her, "Behold, I have given thy brother a thousand pieces of silver; behold, he is to thee a covering of the eyes, unto all them that are with thee and with all others." This was to note that a wife should cast her eyes upon none in a lustful way but her husband; he must be a covering of her eyes unto all who are with her.

HELP 3. Use moderation in meat and drink. Excess in any kind of food greatly provokes unto lust. 2 Peter 2:13–14 says, "They have their eyes full of adultery while they feast with you." This is the reason for Paul's expression in 1 Corinthians 9:26–27: "I, therefore, so run, not as uncertainly; so fight I, not as one that beateth the air, but I keep under my body and bring it into subjection."

HELP 4. If you would keep under fleshly lusts, then make conscience of curbing your thoughts when lust first begins to make entrance there. When a man lets contemplating thoughts lodge in his heart with complacency, it is a thousand to one that they will break out into acts. It is a great provocation to uncleanness for a man to cherish in himself speculative wantonness, to behold in his thoughts some lascivious object. Ezekiel 23:19: "She multiplied her whoredoms in calling to remembrance the days of her youth, wherein she had played the harlot in the land of Egypt." The restraining and curbing of our thoughts is a great help to keep under this sin. "I have made a covenant with my eyes," said Job. He does not then say, "Why therefore should I look upon a maid?" but "Why therefore should I *think* upon a maid?"

HELP 5. If you would mortify and subdue fleshly lusts, use this help: consider that there is a great deal more real evil than there is seeming goodness in this sin of uncleanness. When a harlot would persuade and entice a young man to be unclean with her, she says, as in Proverbs 7:15–17, "I came forth to meet thee, diligently to seek thy face, and I have found thee. I have decked my bed with coverings of tapestry, with carved works, with fine linen of Egypt. I have perfumed my bed with myrrh, aloes and cinnamon." Mark here how she joins together two bitter things and one sweet: "I have perfumed my bed with myrrh, aloes, and cinnamon." Now cinnamon is sweet; the other two are very bitter things, which notes to us that there is twice as much real misery and evil in the sin of uncleanness as there is of seeming joy and delight in it.

HELP 6. Consider seriously and frequently the evil concomitants that attend and accompany this sin of uncleanness.

First, there is thievery in this sin: you rob a body that is not your own. In John 8:4 it is said, "This woman was taken in adultery in the very act." In the original it was "taken in the very theft," to note that adultery is no better than theft. In Proverbs 9:17–18, committing adultery with a woman is called stolen waters: "Stolen waters are sweet and bread eaten in secret is pleasant." This is clearly spoken of a harlot. It continues, "But he knoweth not the dead are there and that her guests are in the depths of hell."

Second, this sin brings infamy and reproach upon a man, too. Proverbs 6:32–33: "He that committeth adultery, a wound and dishonor shall he get, and his reproach shall not be wiped away."

Third, it procures poverty in a man's estate. A man is brought to beggary by it. Proverbs 29:3: "He that keepeth company with harlots spendeth his substance." And Proverbs 6:26: "By means of a whorish woman, a man is brought to a morsel of bread."

Fourth, it will consume your flesh and bones; it will corrupt your blood and weaken your whole man. In Proverbs 5:8, 11 Solomon speaks of a harlot: "Remove thy way far from her and come not near the door of her house, lest thou mourn at last, when thy flesh and thy body are consumed."

Fifth, it makes a man a very magazine of all manner of diseases.

Sixth, it brings stupidity upon the heart. A man who is an unclean man is a stupid sinner and devoid of understanding. Hosea 4:11: "Wine and women take away the heart of a man." Thus I am done with the helps against this first sin of unclean lusts.

But, says another man, "Alas, I would be happy if I had no sin to fear but unclean lusts, but, the Lord be merciful to me, I am troubled with spiritual pride. I cannot live out any grace or perform any duty but I am lifted up with spiritual pride."

I shall give you four helps against the sin of spiritual pride:

HELP 1. Consider that the best of you have a great deal more cause for abasement and humiliation than you have for pride. The best of you have more of sin than of grace in you; as there are more pebbles than diamonds in the quarry and more thorns than roses in the field, so there is more sin than grace in your hearts. Why should you be proud? Though you have many good graces in you, you have a very bad, polluting and sinful nature.

HELP 2. Live in a continual and serious consideration that all the gifts and parts you have, of which you are proud, were all bestowed on you as a gift, as a mere act of donation from God. Now if all the gifts you have were freely given to you of God from His bounty, why then should you be proud of them? Would you think it seemly for a beggar to be proud of the clothes that another man has given him? Just so it is with you: all that you have is mere alms, gifts and acts of grace and mercy from God bestowed upon you. As the Apostle says in 1 Corinthians 4:7, "What hast thou that thou hast not received?" Therefore, this should humble us.

HELP 3. If you would control spiritual pride, consider that, of all things in the world, this is what will most abate and decay your gifts. James 4:6: "The Lord giveth more grace to the humble, but He resisteth the proud." He goes against him as a warrior in battle. He gives grace to a humble heart, not to a proud heart. Therefore take heed of being lifted up in spirit; and, if you are, it should be a matter of great humiliation for you to consider that pride will stifle and strangle grace in your soul. The low valleys are fruitful when the high mountains are barren; so the most humble Christians are most fruitful in grace. Moreover, philosophers give a clear reason for the evil of this sin above others: other vices oppose and fight against their contrary virtues, but pride fights against the whole body of virtue and grace. Other vices oppose their contraries (such as fear opposing hope, sorrow overwhelming joy, covetousness condemning liberality), but pride is a vice that fights against every virtue and every grace.

HELP 4. A great means to mortify and keep under pride in your heart is a serious consideration of the great disproportion there is between God and you, and between yourself and others, and between yourself and yourself.

First, consider the great disproportion there is between God and you, how infinitely He exceeds you. He is like the glorious sun; you are like a clod of dirt. He is the righteous judge of heaven and earth; you are poor, sinful dust and ashes.

Second, consider the great disproportion between yourself and others. It may be that others who have had less time and enjoyed fewer means of grace than you have had are yet a great deal better or proficient in the school of Christ than you are. Therefore, this should abate and keep under your pride.

Third, consider the great disproportion between yourself and yourself. You are proud of the gifts you have now, but, O man, consider what you were in Adam. I am sure that you come far short of the gifts and abilities you had in him. Look upon the disproportion between what you are now and what you were at conversion. It may be that you were then a man full of grace, fervent in prayer, full of affection toward God and zeal for Him; but now your zeal has grown cold and you are dead and formal in duties. Now you want a great many of those graces which you exercised then. You are like some people I have read of who the first year offered gold to their gods, the next year silver, and the third year nothing at all. So you at first were fruitful in grace, and then afterwards you began to wither and decay, and now you are worst of all and yet more proud than ever. I think these considerations should mightily keep under pride in your heart. Now I am done with the second sin, the sin of spiritual pride.

I come now to the third sin of reigning anger, commonly called "passion." Another man may say, "Neither of these two sins troubles me so much. But alas, I am a man of a froward and hasty disposition, and much addicted to passion; therefore, I would gladly know how I might mortify and subdue this sin in me."

I shall give you six rules or directions whereby you may bridle your passions when you are provoked by an injury offered you or the like.

HELP 1. Consider that you have given God greater occasion to be angry with you than ever any man gave you to be angry with him. Should the Lord be strict to mark what you do amiss, and requite every injury done to Him into your bosom, you would have been long ago thrown into hell. Therefore, let this allay and keep under your passions.

HELP 2. Consider that all the injuries that are offered you to provoke and stir up your passion come by the mere providence of God. This was what allayed David's passion when Shimei railed upon him and cursed him. David said, "Let him alone, for God has bidden him do it."

HELP 3. When an occasion of anger is offered, labor to delay and put off the execution of your wrath; let there be some pre-considerations before you execute your wrath and passion. Solomon says in Proverbs 12:16: "A fool's wrath is presently known, but a prudent man covereth his shame." It is a shame to be angry; therefore a wise man will cover and conceal his passion.

HELP 4. Another great help to mortify passion is this: depart out of the company of the man who is angry with you, or who would provoke you to be angry with him. Thus you read (and it is very observable) in 1 Samuel 20:34 that when Saul was angry with Jonathan, Jonathan arose and went out from the presence of his father. Abraham and Lot, because they would not fall out, departed one from another. Solomon says in Proverbs 22:24–25, "Make no friendship with an angry man, and with a furious man thou shalt not go, lest thou learn his ways and get a snare to thy soul." If you are with a furious man, and he snarls at you and you at him, this is the way to increase your passion.

HELP 5. If you would keep under passion, then when any injury or provocation is offered you to be angry, labor to put up with the occasion or injury in silence. Do not utter a multitude of words about it, for in this sense words are wind; and as wind kindles a fire, so words will kindle wrath. Proverbs 26:21: "As coals are to burning coals and wood to fire, so is a contentious man to kindle strife." A multitude of words will provoke to passion; therefore, when you are angry, keep it in and do not utter word after word and reproach after reproach, for that is the way to increase your anger.

HELP 6. To dissuade you from passion, consider that this is a sin that carries many other sins in its womb. Other sins you may commit alone, but you cannot be angry without committing many other sins with it. Proverbs 29:22: "A furious man aboundeth in transgressions." Sometimes pride is mixed with anger and sometimes murder is a consequence of it. According to Genesis 49:6, Simeon and Levi in their anger killed a man. There is an abundance of sins wrapped up in the womb of anger, and this danger, if considered, may be a great help to suppress and keep it under.

And thus I have done with particular helps against those three particular sins, which I hope, if seriously considered, may be of some use and benefit in mortifying them. I have a word or two by way of use to wind up all that has been said touching this doctrine of mortification, and then I shall conclude the text. The uses that I shall make shall be only to give you five plain cautions or directions about this doctrine.

CAUTION 1. When you have subdued and mortified one sin, be sure to expect another to rise in its place. Beloved, a Christian's life is a continual warfare. He must combat with spiritual wickedness in high places. The devil will never let you alone; if one temptation does not prevail, another shall. When one lust or corruption is mortified, another will presently rise up in place of it. Therefore, you must continually stand on your guard. That is the first thing by way of counsel.

CAUTION 2. Content not yourselves with a small beginning of mortification. Many men, because they have a cessation of their lusts, therefore think they are mortified. Some are contented with a mutation of their lusts. They have been young adulterers and now they are old worldlings; therefore they are satisfied, and some are content because they play and jest with their lusts as fencers. They pretend to kill their lusts but never hurt them.

CAUTION 3. Take this caution when you are about to mortify sin: Be sure that you bend the chief part of your strength against your bosom sins, your master sins. Where sin makes the greatest incursions upon your soul, there make the greatest opposition and resistance. Do not do as Saul did with the Amalekites in 1 Samuel 15:9: he spared Agag their king and the best of the sheep and oxen and all that was good and would not utterly destroy them. Many men kill their ordinary corruptions, but spare and indulge their great and master and beloved sins.

CAUTION 4. Labor that your mortification reaches to inward and secret evils as well as to gross and palpable sins. Inward and secret sins are most dangerous, and are harder to discern and decry in the soul than greater sins. Oh, my beloved, when there are whole swarms of inward lusts that you never mind, and take no pains to subdue and no care to suppress and keep under, you do not perform half the work of mortification.

CAUTION 5. Lastly, in mortifying your corruptions, take Christ's strength along with you; for you are not able to do it of yourselves. Therefore, beg His help and assistance in whom you shall be enabled to do all things. "If you through the Spirit do mortify the deeds of the body, you shall live."

The Right Hearing of Sermons

The Right Hearing of Sermons

The Hearer's Duty

"But he said, 'Yea, rather blessed are they that hear the Word of God and keep it.' " Luke 11:28

In the humanity of Jesus Christ such a luster and beauty shone and broke forth that, even in such a despicable person as He was deemed to be, yet the very words that He spoke and the works that He did declared Him to be the Son of God. In John 7:46 His very enemies confessed that never did a man speak as Christ spoke. He spoke better than ever man spoke. By the words He delivered it was evident that He was more than man, but the works that He did also spoke plainly and with an audible voice His divinity. And concerning the miracles which He wrought, it was said of many of them that never was it thus done since the beginning of the world. His miracles wrought admiration even in the hearts of those men in whom they wrought envy and malice against Him. The miracle recounted in Luke 11, the chapter from which our text is taken—the dispossessing of a dumb man of the devil—spread fame and renown of Christ through many parts of the world. And though His enemies were obstinante (in that they would not, notwithstanding these miracles that He wrought, acknowledge His divinity), yet there was a young woman who slipped out and went to Christ, and lifted up her voice saluting Him in these words: "Blessed is the womb that bare Thee, and the paps that gave Thee suck." And had this commendation been given to another, it might have made him proud, but it worked the contrary effect upon Christ. He gave her a rebuke rather than any thanks, and told her that rather blessed are they who hear the Word of God and keep it. And thus I have brought you to the words of my text.

But before I come to give you the doctrine which the words will afford, give me leave to speak something concerning the young woman saluting Christ after this manner. The words that she spoke were a common proverb among the Jews. When any man had done a commendable thing that was excellent and extraordinary, they would immediately cry out to him, "Blessed is the womb that bare thee and the paps that gave thee suck." From whence I would note this much: Good children are a great blessing to and commendation to their parents.

And hence it is that you read so often in the Scriptures what a blessing it is for a father to be the father of a good son and for a mother to be the mother of a good child—for example, in Proverbs 10:1 and 15:20—and, on the contrary, what a great curse it is for parents to bring forth wicked children into the world. A wicked child is a shame to his father, and a heaviness to his mother who brought him into the world.

I would have you make this use of this doctrine: You who have good children, who are instruments of the praise and glory of God, bless His name for them. And you who have bad children, look upon it as a stroke of God's heavy hand upon you.

But this is only a point by the way, from the woman speaking thus of Christ: "Blessed is the womb that bare Thee, and the paps that gave Thee suck." But Christ told her, "Rather blessed are they that hear the Word of God and keep it." Christ says "rather blessed." He does not say that the woman who bore Him was not blessed, for she bore Him in her heart as well as in her womb; but Christ spoke this with a gentle and loving rebuke to the woman who gave him the commendation. Said Christ, "You cry out, 'Blessed is the womb that bare Thee,' but I say, 'Blessed are they who hear the Word of God and keep it.' " So note from Christ's example here that you must take a great deal of heed that you be not tickled with pride whenever you hear yourselves commended. You see here that Christ would give no assent to their commendation of His mother.

And then, again, "Yea, rather blessed." Christ said that those are "rather blessed" who hear the Word of God and keep it than His mother who brought Him into the world. From whence observe that a believer who hears and obeys Christ is more blessed in so doing than the virgin Mary was in merely bringing Jesus Christ into the world, though it was the happiest birth that ever woman brought forth.

And, oh, how should this be a spur to hearers to make them obey and practice what they hear! But I shall keep you no longer in the entrance into the words, and therefore I shall only give you something to note from the manner of the expression that Christ here uses, and then draw out the doctrine the words will afford. In the form of speech that Christ here uses, observe it is not said, "Blessed are they who *hear* the Word of God." There are many sorts of hearers who come short of blessing, but "Blessed are they who hear the Word of God and *keep* it."

There are four sorts of hearers spoken of in Matthew 13. Three of them are bad and but one good, that one who hears the Word of God aright. All who hear the Word do not obtain a blessing.

Again, it is not said, "Blessed are they who hear", but "Blessed are they who hear and *keep* what they hear."

It is not said, "Blessed are they who believe." Observe that, though it is true, yet it is not said so, lest men should think that a bare and naked believing is enough to entitle them to blessedness. There are many men who pretend to have faith and assurance, and yet live above duties, above hearing and praying. Therefore Christ does not say, "Blessed are they who believe," but "Blessed are they who hear the Word and keep it."

It is not also said, "Blessed are they who keep the Word in a disjunction from hearing," but "Blessed are they who keep the Word in conjunction with hearing. Blessed are you who hear and keep the Word." There are many men pretending to be advanced in their practice and in keeping what Christ commands, but it is disjunctive obedience. They will not hear. Those are only blessed, in Christ's esteem, who keep and hear the Word of God.

It is not said here in the text, "Blessed *shall* they be who hear and keep the Word of God," but "Blessed *are* they who hear and keep the Word." You shall not only be a blessed man when you come into heaven, but you *are* a blessed man while you are upon the earth. "You have your fruit unto holiness, and the end of everlasting life" (Romans 6:22).

Observe further, it is not said, "Blessed are they who hear and keep it," but "Blessed are they who hear the *Word of God* and keep it." For you may hear errors and blasphemies and keep them, and be accursed for so doing; but "Blessed are they who hear the Word of God and keep it." And this should teach men to take heed *how* they hear and *what* they hear, and that they hear nothing but that which is the Word of God. We read of some who will follow teachers who bring in "damnable heresies" (2 Peter 2:1). Many shall follow their sensuality. Now such as these are not blessed, who hear men who bring errors and heresies, but they are cursed rather.

Observe further that Christ does not say, "Rather blessed are they who hear My sayings and keep them," but they who hear God's Word. For had Christ said, "Rather blessed are they who hear My words," the people might have been ready to think that Christ entailed blessedness to His own preaching, and to those who heard Christ teach here upon the earth. But, said He, "Blessed are they who hear the Word of God, be it from Paul or Apollos or Timothy or Titus, or any minister of Christ to the world's end. Whoever shall hear the Word of God contained in the Scriptures, preached out of their mouths, and shall keep and obey it, they are more blessed than My mother who bore me is blessed for the sole reason of bringing Me into the world."

In this very expression a secret glory is put upon the ministers of the Word, and this is the reason for that saying of Scripture: he who believes shall do greater works than Christ did (John 14:12). That is, he who ministers shall convert more souls than ever Christ did. It is true that Christ might (if He had so pleased) have converted every man who heard Him, but He would not lest men should thereby have undervalued His ministers, and have thought that none could convert souls but Christ. And therefore there were more converted by Peter and other apostles than by Christ Himself, so that He might hereby encourage men to hear ordinary ministers.

There were some in the church of Corinth, according to 1 Corinthians 1:12, who said, "We are for Paul"; others, "We are for Apollos"; others, "We are for Cephas"; and others, "We are for Christ." Now the Apostle blames those too who said, "I am of Christ." There were some among them who said, "I care not for hearing Paul, or Apollos, or Cephas; I will hear Jesus Christ." It was a vanity in them to undervalue the ministry of Paul and Apollos, and so claim to be exalting Christ. It is a sinful exalting of Christ to denigrate Paul and Apollos. And so in these times for men to exalt Christ and yet denigrate the ministry is as sinful now as it was in the apostles' time. And therefore Christ Himself was careful to preserve the honor of the ministry that was to succeed Him to the end of the world: "Blessed are they that hear the Word of God and keep it."

It is not said, "Rather blessed are they for hearing and for keeping the Word," but "Blessed are they that hear the Word of God and keep it."

Blessed doers never come with a *for,* but only with an *if* or a *that.* The Lord does not bless you for your hearing, though you should hear as many sermons as there are days; but He blesses those who hear and practice what they hear. Hearing the Word and practicing and obeying it are the qualifications or characteristic notes of such persons as shall be blessed by Christ, but not the causes of their blessedness.

And thus I have given you these marks from the form of speech Christ here uses. I shall now explain the words a little more to you, "Blessed are they that hear the Word of God and keep it."

QUESTION. What is meant here by keeping the Word you hear?

ANSWER. You must know that there is a double keeping of the Word, the one in your memories and the one in your practice.

1. *There is a keeping the Word in your memories.* This you have illustrated in Luke 2:19. It is said there that "Mary *kept* these things, and pondered them in her heart." Our memories should be like the ark wherein the pot of manna was kept. The Word of God should be treasured up in our memories as the pot of manna was in the ark. But this is not the keeping spoken of in our text, for there are many men who keep the Word in their memories and yet never practice it in their lives

2. *There is a keeping the Word in your practice.* This is when you have a conscientious care to sway your practice according to what you hear and know; and

this is the keeping that is here meant. "Blessed are they that hear the Word of God and keep it," that is, keep it in their practice, and keep it and make conscience to do what they hear and know.

The words being thus opened, the observation from them will be this: they are rather blessed who hear the Word of God, and practice what they hear, than the mother of Jesus Christ was for bringing Him into the world.

Beloved, it is a point that, I confess, had it not been in the Bible, would have been incredible: that those who hear the Word and keep it should be more blessed than she was who bore Christ in her womb. That Christ should put a "rather blessed" upon you, O man or woman who hear the Word of God and keep it, than upon the virgin Mary for bearing Christ into the world—what a great privilege is this!

Beloved, it is worth your noting what a different dialect is used between this woman here in the text, and Elizabeth, who was a cousin to the virgin Mary. This woman in the text cried out, "Blessed is the womb that bare Thee, and the paps that gave Thee suck." But Elizabeth said, "Blessed is she that believed" (Luke 1:45). If the virgin Mary had not borne Christ in her heart as well as in her womb, she would not have been a blessed woman.

Before I give you the reasons for the point, I shall only draw this inference from it to confute the dotage of the Church of Rome that dotes so much upon the virgin Mary. Where they have one service for the glory of Christ, they have twenty for the glory of the virgin Mary. They would have the world believe that she was without sin. If that is so, why would Christ pronounce others rather blessed than she? This, then, is the confutation of the Church of Rome, that holds that the virgin Mary had no original sin. If this were so, then she would have been more blessed than anyone else in the world. And if that is true, then this text must be false, for Christ said here, "Rather blessed are they that hear the Word of God and keep it than she."

This confutes them because they so lift up the righteousness, holiness and dignity of the virgin Mary that they undervalue the righteousness of Jesus Christ her Son. They so dote upon the virgin Mary that they make her the great mediator for us to the Father, whereas we maintain that Christ is the only Mediator: "for there is but one Mediator between God and man, the Man Christ Jesus" (1 Timothy 2:5).

Ministers had never more need to confute popish doctrines and opinions than now. For never was popery more likely to increase and flourish in this land than it is now; and therefore I rather give these glances concerning them because there is great danger, lest the people be infected with these popish fooleries. I speak this upon my own experience. I have been a preacher these ten years, and in all that time I never perceived so much inclining towards popery as I have done during these two months. Since these late, strange actions that have been done among us, I have seen many stagger about our religion and become strongly tempted to embrace and fall into popery, which is the reason that induced me to make this digression.

Now let us turn to the reason why those who hear and keep the Word are more blessed than even the mother of Jesus:

1. Christ counts such in a nearer relation to Him than His own relatives. In Mark 3:33-35, when Christ was told that His mother and brothers were out seeking Him, He said, "Who is My mother or brethren? Whosoever shall hear the Word of God and keep it, the same is My brother, My sister, and mother."

2. If you hear the Word of God and keep what you hear, you shall persevere and have the end of your faith. In Matthew 7:24–25, Christ says, "Whosoever hears these sayings of Mine and does them, I will liken him to a wise man which buildedst his house upon a rock, and the rain descended and the floods came, and the winds beat upon that house, and it fell not, for it was founded upon a rock." So those only who hear the Word of God and practice it shall have the end of their faith, and have their souls built upon the rock of Jesus Christ that shall never be removed.

3. You are blessed in practicing what you hear, because thereby you may bring many others to blessedness. In 1 Peter 3:1, the Apostle says, "Wives, be in subjection to your own husbands, that if any obey not the Word, they may without a word be won by the conversation of their wives." And those men who have been won by your good example, when they come to appear before God in judgment, shall glorify God in the day of their visitation, and shall bless God that by your means they were brought to heaven.

4. They who practice what they hear are blessed because, though they may not bring others to heaven, yet they are sure to come to heaven themselves. Revelation 14:12–13 says, "Here is the perseverance of the saints, who keep the commandments of God and their faith in Jesus. Blessed are the dead in the Lord; they rest from their labors, for their deeds follow them." Those who keep the commandments of God and their faith in Jesus shall come themselves to heaven, though they bring no one else with them. Where a gospel life goes before, an angel's life shall follow after. You who lead gospel lives here assure yourselves that you shall lead angels' lives hereafter. And therefore make conscience to do and practice what you hear and know.

We come now to the application, and the use that I shall make of it shall be threefold, for lamentation, consolation, and exhortation.

USE OF LAMENTATION. Is it so that they are rather blessed who hear and practice what they hear in the Word than the virgin Mary? Oh, then, how should this consideration provoke you to lamentation, that when you may have blessing upon such terms as these, "Hear My words and make conscience to practice it, and you shall be blessed," yet you reject your own mercy. Oh, you perverse and hard-hearted man or woman, who will not practice what you hear, you reject your own mercy!

And to set home this particular upon your own hearts, give me leave to press it with these three considerations.

CONSIDERATION 1. Consider that you who do not make conscience to practice what you hear provoke the Lord to take the Word away from you so that you shall not hear it at all. Amos 8:5–11: "When Israel was weary of the Word of God and of His sabbaths, saying, 'When will the new moon be gone, that we may sell corn, and the sabbath that we may set forth wheat?' " God said, "I will cause the sun to go down at noon, and will darken the earth in the clear day; and I will send a famine in the land, not a famine of bread, or a thirst for water, but of hearing the words of the Lord."

God may take the Word away from you for not profiting from it. Matthew 21:43: "The kingdom of God shall be taken away from you and given to a nation bringing forth the fruits thereof."

CONSIDERATION 2. Consider that your hearing, if you do not practice what you hear, will aggravate your damnation in another way. In John 15:22 Christ says, "If I had not come and spoken unto them, they had not had sin; but now they have no cloak for their sin." So in Luke 12:47: "That servant that knew his lord's will and prepared not himself, neither did according to his will, shall be beaten with many stripes."

It has been observed regarding the book of Isaiah that, from the 13th to the 24th chapter of that prophecy, we read of many dismal denunciations of judgment: the burden of Babylon, the burden of Tyre, and of Moab, and of Egypt, and the burden of the desert of the sea. The Lord commanded the prophet to pronounce a burdensome prophecy against many nations and people; but among them all there was the burden of the valley of vision in Isaiah 22. And it is observed that this is the most burdensome of them all, and the reason is that this was the place of vision and knowledge, where the Word of God was dispensed, and because of the people's sinfulness and unprofitableness. Their burden is heavier than all the rest because it is the burden of the valley of the vision. Though other men may go to hell who live in those parts of the world where the Word was never taught, and where they never heard the voice of the glad tidings of salvation sounding in their ears, yet those who live where the gospel is preached, and know the truth and yet do not walk answerably, shall go to hell with a heavier burden than the others shall.

CONSIDERATION 3. Another consideration is that you are devoid of the love of God; you love Him not, nor He you, if you do not make conscience to practice what you hear. 1 John 2:4–5: "Whosoever keeps His Word, in him the love of God has been truly perfected; and he that says he knows Him and keeps not His Word is a liar, and the truth is not in him."

USE OF EXHORTATION. I shall now speak something by way of exhortation to provoke you all, in the fear of God, to make conscience to practice what you hear and know. And to this end consider that God looks upon all your knowledge and profession to be worthless unless you practice what you know and profess. God looks upon all your hearing and praying as nothing unless your conversation is answerable to it. And is it not a pity that for want of practice you should lose the blessing of all your hearing, and make it of no worth or esteem in God's account; that though you have a great deal of notional knowledge, yet He looks upon you as ignorant, and upon you who have heard so many sermons as if you have never heard one all your lifetime? It is said of the sons of Eli that they knew not the Lord. Why them? Surely they knew Him! But because they were sons of Belial, and unholy and profane in their lives, therefore God did not account their knowledge and gifts to be anything because they did not practice what they knew. Oh, then, beloved, shall God account your hearing as nothing and your praying as nothing because you do not make conscience to practice what you hear and know?

You can have no persuasion in your own soul of the love of God towards you unless you make conscience to practice what you hear. In John 14:15 Christ says, "If you love Me, keep My commandments." And therefore often in Scripture these two are put together: loving God and keeping His commandments.

USE OF CONSOLATION. But now, by way of consolation, I think I hear a poor soul ask, "Are they only blessed who hear the Word of God and keep what they hear? Who, then, shall be blessed, for who is able to keep what he hears? I many times hear a duty commanded, but am not able to perform it, and such and such things required, but I am not able to keep them, and I am urged to obtain such and such graces, but I am not able to get them."

For your comfort, know that if you lived under a covenant of works, you could never be a blessed man, for you are not able to perform the conditions of it. For that requires you to keep and fulfill the whole law of God perfectly and personally. But now, since under a covenant of grace, God accepts your keeping of the law if it is done sincerely though it is done but imperfectly. And though it is not done in your own person, yet if it is done in the person of another, the Lord accepts it.

God says to us under a covenant of grace, "Believe and live. If you make conscience to keep the Word, though you cannot keep it, yet I will pardon you and accept you. And though you cannot keep the law in your own person, yet if My Son keeps it for you, I will accept His obedience as if it were done by you."

And therefore you must not lie down under despondency of mind, because you are not under a covenant of works but under a covenant of grace, wherein Christ accepts sincere obedience though it is not perfect.

Know for your comfort that if you have had a full purpose of heart to keep that which you hear, it is looked upon by God as if you kept it. Hebrews 11:17 says that "by faith Abraham, when he was tried, did offer up his son Isaac," because Abraham did, in resolution and purpose of his heart, determine to obey God in offering up his son. Therefore the Scripture looks upon it as done, though it was only in purpose, not in actuality.

In the same way, with regard to you who are the sons of Abraham, and have the faith of Abraham, those holy duties which you desire to perform better—such as to pray better, to hear better, and to practice and live better than you do—in divine account these are looked upon as if they were really done.

Directions for Profitable Hearing

"Take heed therefore how you hear." Luke 8:18

Beloved, it shall be my care and endeavor to provide such able and godly men to exercise every morning as may be acceptable to you, and let it be your care to bring along hearts suitable to the work. I shall take care *what* you hear; it is your work to take heed *how* you hear.

"Take heed, therefore, how you hear."

We are to take heed not only what and whom we hear, but also how we hear.

In the words there are these two parts:

1. A serious caution given by Christ: "take heed how you hear."

2. A reason for this caution expressed in this word: "therefore, take heed how you hear."

Why?

Because there is nothing hidden that shall not be revealed. As we see your faces, so Christ sees your hearts, and observes all the deviations and miscarriages thereof in your approaches to Him and waiting upon Him in the duties of His service. "Take heed therefore how you hear."

From the caution that Christ here gives we may observe that Christians must take heed not only of the person whom and the matter what they hear, but also the manner how they hear the Word of God.

From the reason for the caution observe further that the consideration of the all-seeing eye of God, who sees and takes notice of your behavior in your addresses to Him, should incite and provoke you to take heed of the manner how you hear the Word of God. The all-seeing eye of God should be a motive to restrain us from the least secret sin. As Job said, "I made a covenant with my eyes; why then should I think to look upon a maid? For does not the Lord see all my ways and count all my steps?" (Job 31:1, 4).

But I shall not tarry upon these things, but shall only speak something to you practically from the words. And the doctrine I shall insist upon shall be the very words of my text, and then there shall be no need to multiply any more passages to prove it.

DOCTRINE. Christians ought to take heed how or in what manner they hear the Word of God.

The reasons I shall lay down for the proof of this doctrine shall be these five, being none other than what is found in this parable. For this counsel here given by Christ is but a conclusion to the preceding parable of the four sorts of hearers, wherein, to wind up all, our Savior gives caution that we should take heed how we hear. From this parable we shall draw these five reasons to enforce this doctrine:

1. Most hearers in the world hear amiss; therefore we should take heed how we hear. There is but one sort in four who hears the Word of God aright, and if a great many, nay most of men, miscarry in hearing the Word, therefore let us take heed.

2. Another reason given in the parable is that the devil takes a great deal of heed to interrupt you

in hearing, and therefore you should take heed how you hear. In the 12th verse of this chapter, when the seed was sown, the devil came and took the Word out of their hearts lest they should believe and be saved. Now is the devil so careful to interrupt and hinder the efficacious working of the Word upon the heart, and shall there be no care in you to attend upon God without distraction when you come into His presence? The devil hinders us in hearing the Word of God as he did the "sons of God" in Job 2:1. It is said that when they came before the Lord, Satan came in the midst of them. So when we come into the presence of God to hear His Word, the devil stands at our right hand to divert and distract our thoughts from attending upon it. In Genesis 15:11 it is said that when Abraham was offering up a sacrifice to God the fowls of the air came down and picked upon it. This represents (says Diodicus) the frequent disturbances the people of God meet with from Satan to distract and interrupt them in the duties and services they are about. "Take heed therefore how you hear."

3. You must take heed how you hear because, if you do not, the Word will not only be ineffectual to you, but will do you a great deal of hurt. This you have laid down in the 16th verse. "No man," said Christ, "when he has lit a candle covers it with a vessel." This text does not refer to the preachers of the Word. It is not meant of their light; but it refers to hearers of the Word. Now, says Christ, the light which they have must not be hidden under a vessel or under a bed. From whence one well observes that if a light or a candle is put under a bed, not only the

room where it is lacks light, but the bed and the man who lies in it are in danger of burning. So that man who lives under the means of grace and the dispensations of the Word, and takes no care how he hears it, is like a man who puts a candle under his bed and is in as great a danger of hellfire as the other is of being burned by a temporal fire.

4. Take heed how you hear, because the great God's all-seeing and heart-searching eye takes notice of the carriages of your hearts and the behavior of your spirits while you are hearing. If the Apostle, in 1 Corinthians 11:10, makes the presence of angels an argument why the Corinthian women should wear a veil in token of their subjection to their husbands ("for this cause ought the woman to have a covering over her head, because of the angels"), then much more ought we to take heed how we hear, not only because the angels of heaven are present in the assemblies of the saints when they come to worship God, but because the God of the angels takes notice of the frame of your hearts and the deportment of your spirits when you are before Him. This reason you have laid down in the 17th verse of this chapter: "for nothing is secret that shall not be made manifest, neither anything hid that shall not be made known."

5. Another reason is that God dispenses His blessings according to the conscientious care we express in hearing His Word. And this is laid down in the words of the text: "Take heed therefore how you hear; for whosoever has, to him shall be given, and whosoever has not, from him shall be taken away even that which he seems to have."

USE. I shall now speak something practical, by way of use, to what has been said and so conclude. And that I may set home this counsel that our Savior here gives us, I shall lay down to you these seven particular directions.

1. Take heed how you hear. Take heed that you hear the Word of God preparedly. As the preacher must take care to find acceptable words, so the people should labor to bring acceptable affections to the work. In the sanctuary there was on one side a table of shewbread, representing the tribes of Israel, and a candlestick on the other side to symbolize the service of God, and the incense in the middle which is prayer, to note that when we come to the service of God we should hear with all attention and pray with affection.

2. Hear the Word not only preparedly, but attentively, too, as those did in Acts 8:6. It is said that the people with one accord gave heed unto those things that Philip spoke. And so in Nehemiah 8:5–6, when Ezra opened the book of the Law and read in the sight of all the people, they all stood up; and when he blessed the Lord, the great God, all the people answered "Amen, amen," lifting up their hands. In Luke 19:48 it is said that all the people were attentive to hear Christ. Therefore, those who hear the Word with gazing eyes, wandering thoughts, and sleepy bodies cannot hear it attentively, but are to be reproved. Let them take heed that, while they hear the Word so remissly and so sleepily, the devil does not catch them napping. Let such hearers read the story of Eutychus in Acts 20:9 and tremble. And so likewise are they to be reproved who hear the Word

with an unquiet demeanor, walking from place to place. It is said in Nehemiah 8:7 that when Ezra read the book of the Law, all the people stood in their own place.

3. Hear the Word of God retentively. Labor to keep in your memory what you hear, that you may put it into practice for your life. For hearing is not merely for hearing's sake, but for practice's sake. Your heart should be as the ark was. As that was a repository to keep the pot of manna in, so this manna, the Word of God, should be treasured up in your heart. In Luke 8:15 the good hearer hears the Word of God with an honest and good heart and keeps it. So in Isaiah 42:23 the prophet says, "Who among you will give ear to this? Who will hearken and hear for the time to come?" Who will treasure up the Word for the time to come, for later ages, so that the Word may have a continual impression upon your hearts?

4. Hear the Word understandingly. Christ called the multitude and bade them hear and understand. As the palate tastes and distinguishes between different meats, so the ear should distinguish doctrines, as in Job 12:11: "Does not the ear try words, and the mouth taste his meat?" In Hebrews 5:14 the Apostle said, "Those that are of full age have their senses exercised to discern both good and evil," and to know when the Word is soundly and practically preached. Men should not be like a sponge under a sermon, to suck in all they hear indifferently; but they must with understanding search the Scriptures to see whether those things are so or not which are delivered to them. Mercer, commenting upon the

passage from Job, made a good observation that the original word for an ear signifies a pair of balances, so as to point out that, when we are hearing, we should be weighing. We should not only use the touchstone to try whether it is true or not, but also the balance, whether it is of weight or not. If men should weigh all the doctrines of our times in the balance of the sanctuary, how many would be found light?

5. Hear the Word applicatively. If a patient has never such excellent counsel given him, never so powerful a medicine prescribed, if he does not apply it, it will do him no more good than if he had never known it. And beloved, there is not one among us but may apply to his own soul what he hears preached and delivered out of the Word. For example, if the most foul and enormous sin is reproved, say to yourself, "Either I have been, or am, or may be guilty of that sin; or if the crime is such as neither I have, nor do, nor will commit, yet if God should leave me to myself, I would be guilty of it." Therefore hear the Word applicatively, and say with David, "I will hear what the Lord will say to me."

6. Hear the Word of God reverentially. Because our God is a consuming fire, not only the wicked but the people of God likewise should look upon God with such apprehensions as these. Many people represent God to themselves in such familiar notions that they ultimately breed a concept of God which we ought not to have. Rather consider that our God is a consuming fire, and therefore let us serve Him with reverence and godly fear. It is true that we may, and ought, through Christ draw near to

God with confidence, as to a father, but withal we must demean ourselves with a humble reverence in His presence.

7. You must hear the Word of God obediently. Come with an obedient heart ready, prepared, and disposed to stoop and submit to all the instructions, corrections, and reproofs of the Word of God, like those spoken of in Acts 10:33: "We are all here present before God to hear all the things that are commanded you of God." Such a frame and disposition of heart should you always bring with you when you come to hear the Word of God. Be willing to submit to it, and, if you had a thousand necks, to lay them all under the obedience of the Word. A learned Dutch divine once said, "Hear the Word with fear." We read of an obedient ear. Why? The ear is for hearing, but the meaning is that we must hear to obey.

APPLICATION. Is this so, that we must take heed how we hear?

1. Then, by way of exhortation, take heed that you do not come unprepared. Take heed lest you come with ungodly and unhumble hearts into God's presence.

2. Take heed that you do not come to hear the Word carpingly. There are many in these times who come to hear merely to carp and entrap the minister if they can. They forget all the good matter of the sermon, but if there is anything amiss or impertinently (as they conceive) delivered, they will be sure to focus upon that, though they let slip all the rest.

3. Do not hear the Word dependingly, that is, as

if your salvation is determined by this obedience. Do not depend upon your hearing or praying or any other service. You must make your duties your *way*, not your Christ. Many times the Lord interrupts and keeps off the force and efficacy of His Word from the hearer because he depends too much upon the hearing of the Word or the preacher of it. When the Israelites fought with the Philistines and had the worst of it, they imputed their loss to the absence of the ark from them; but when they had the ark with them, they had worse success than before. And a learned divine gives this reason for it: that they idolized the ark and depended too much upon it.

Therefore, in hearing the Word of God, do not depend too much upon your own strength, or upon the man, or upon the matter he preaches; for though the matter is good, yet this is the way to have the benefit and profit of it diverted from you. In prayer we should so prepare ourselves for that duty as if we had no Spirit in heaven to help our infirmities; but when we have performed the duty we should look upon ourselves as if we had never said a word, but as if Christ had prayed in us and done all in all for us. So when we have heard a sermon, we should look up to Christ and beg His blessing upon it that it may not return void, but accomplish the work for which it was sent and be powerful and efficacious for the good of our souls.

4. Take heed how you hear, and be persuaded in the Lord to practice this rule, upon this ground: because the Lord proportions out His blessings with the Word answerable to your care in hearing it.

The Lord requires in us an answerable care in

the use of means to increase those graces in us for which He has appointed those means. "With what measure you mete, it shall be measured to you again" (Luke 6:38). Sometimes it is applied to justice: as you judge others, so God shall judge you; sometimes to works of mercy: "Give full measure running over, for with what measure you mete it shall be meted to you again." God shall restore to you again answerable to your charity towards others.

But another evangelist, citing Christ's words, applies this phrase to the hearing of the Word: "Take heed how you hear, for with what measure you mete it shall be meted to you again" (Mark 4:24). That is, as you measure the Word in your preparation for it before you come to hear it, so God will mete out to you your profit and benefit by it after you have heard it. The efficacy and profit of the Word upon your hearts shall be answerable to your preparation and care in receiving it. "Take heed therefore how you hear."